BACKYARD BIRD GUIDES

Identifying
and Feeding Birds

BACKYARD BIRD GUIDES

Identifying
and Feeding Birds
Bill Thompson III

HOUGHTON MIFFLIN HARCOURT PUBLISHING COMPANY
BOSTON NEW YORK

For information about permission to reproduce selections from this book, write to Permissions, Houghton Mifflin Harcourt Publishing Company, 215 Park Avenue South, New York, New York 10003.

www.hmhco.com

Library of Congress Cataloging-in-Publication Data

Thompson, Bill, date.
 Identifying and feeding birds / Bill Thompson III.
   p. cm. — (Peterson field guides/Bird Watcher's Digest backyard
 bird guides ; 1)
 Includes index.
 ISBN 978-0-618-90444-0
   1. Bird attracting—North America. 2. Birds—Feeding and feeds—North
America. 3. Birds—North America—Identification. I. Title.
 QL676.57.N7T46 2010
 598.072'347—dc22   2010007859

Book design by George Restrepo

Printed in China
SCP 10 9 8 7 6 5 4

To all the birds that have graced my feeders
during the past four decades:
you have enriched my life immensely.

Contents

Acknowledgments

MANY PEOPLE HELPED SHAPE MY EXPERIENCES attracting wild birds, which in turn helped formulate the content in this book.

My fellow bird watchers in the West shared their insight and experiences, which helped me augment the scope of this book: Linda Beutler, Miles Blumhardt, Tami Bulow, Kevin J. Cook, Lynn Hassler, Alvaro Jaramillo, Durrae Johanek, Liz Payne, John Riutta, Bill Schmoker, and Amy Stewart.

To my parents, Bill and Elsa Thompson, for letting birds flit into our lives.

To my wife, Julie Zickefoose, for sharing many wonderful years of bird watching with me, along with her immense knowledge.

To Phoebe and Liam, for also keeping their eyes on the birds, and for putting up with their parents' long birding trips and intense focus on all things avian. Kids, you had no choice but to become birders too.

To Pat Murphy, for being my first birding mentor, and for the gift of a homemade peanut feeder.

To Mary Beacom Bowers, for teaching me the ropes of editing and writing.

At Houghton Mifflin Harcourt, special thanks go to Lisa A. White, the finest editor a writer could have (and a darn good bird watcher herself!). I also thank Teresa Elsey, Katrina Kruse, Tim Mudie, Elizabeth Pierson, George Restrepo, and Taryn Roeder.

At *Bird Watcher's Digest,* my deepest thanks to the staff for keeping things under control when I am on a book-writing deadline. They are Jim Cirigliano, Claire Mullen, Ann Kerenyi, Chris Blondel, Helen Neuberger, Katherine Koch, Diane Busch, Susan Hill, Melanie Singer, and of course my brother, Andy Thompson (*BWD* publisher), and sister, Laura Fulton, plus Elsa Catbird Thompson, the only person to have worked for *BWD* since its inception. And to Dad, for helping to start this whole thing.

Thanks to my literary agent, Russell Galen, for his support, amazing skill, and insight.

And a very special thanks to the readers of *Bird Watcher's Digest,* who have trusted me and the *BWD* staff to send them a magazine full of birds and words for more than 30 years.

Introduction

DOES THE WORLD REALLY NEED ANOTHER BOOK about bird feeding? The last time I checked, there were more than 2,720,000 search-engine results for "bird feeding book." So one might argue that we've reached saturation in this genre.

You'll be the ultimate judge, but I'd like to think that this one is different. How is it different? Well, I'm going to let you in on a little secret: *bird feeding is NOT hard to do.*

It's true.

Doing it right and getting the most satisfaction out of bird feeding requires equal measures of knowledge, effort, and patience—plus a willingness to experiment. I hope to share with you in these pages all of the insider tips, tricks, and know-how I've accumulated in 30 years of feeding birds. And I'll help you avoid making the same mistakes I've made (some of them multiple times).

I've been watching birds since I was six or seven years old, and I'm now entering my fourth decade as a bird watcher. If you believe my grandmother Thompson, my first word was *junco,* which I uttered at the age of 18 months while eating oatmeal in a highchair looking out at her snow-covered bird feeder. That could just be a bit of Thompson family lore, like the "fact" that our weird second toes show that we are descended from royalty!

Estimates of the number of bird watchers in North America vary: some studies indicate there are 90 million of us, while others put the number closer to 50 million. Either way, there are a lot of bird enthusiasts out there, and most of us feed birds in our backyards or on our decks—somewhere where we can watch them.

Over my decades of bird watching, I've stopped feeding birds only a few times—when I lived in large metropolitan areas. And I really missed it. Feeding birds is one of the most enjoyable activities we can do. But we should always remember that it's done more for us than for the birds. Scientific studies have shown that our native birds do not really and truly need the food at our feeding stations to survive. It's true that some species have expanded their ranges thanks to the always-available food at our bird feeders. However, birds are adaptable creatures that have evolved through the eons to find food and to survive on their own.

Knowing (as we do now) that we feed birds so we can enjoy them up close, we also need to understand that we owe it to our avian friends to feed them responsibly. By this I do not mean simply that we feed them the proper foods in the correct feeders (though we will certainly talk about that in this book). Rather, I mean that we need to make sure our backyards—feeders and all—are safe for birds. If we leave our feeders full of old, moldy seed or let our birdbaths get green with algae, we're doing more harm than good for our birds.

In my years as a birding guide, as a lecturer on the bird festival circuit, and as a bird book author, I've frequently used the catch phrase *See more birds, have more fun.* In fact it's something of a mantra for my approach to birds, bird watchers, and birding.

For this book, let's tweak that catch phrase a bit to: *Feed more birds, have more fun.*

Now, are you ready to have some fun?

— BILL THOMPSON III
APRIL 2010, WHIPPLE, OHIO

Identifying
and Feeding Birds

Chapter 1
The Bird-friendly Backyard

Birds: What's Not to Like?

BIRDS HAVE ALWAYS FASCINATED HUMANS. It has to do with how much we humans identify with birds. Think about it: Birds sing beautiful songs. They come in a spectrum of colors—some gaudy, some subtly beautiful. They form strong and loyal pair and family bonds. They have interesting behavior. And most can fly—which, thanks to the Wright brothers, we humans have now been doing for slightly more than 100 years. Feeding brings these fascinating creatures right to our windowsills and deck railings, allowing us to gaze into their wild eyes. It's not too much of a stretch to believe that birds and humans have a bond that goes back thousands of years.

BUNTINGS can be attracted to feeders with millet or mixed seed. These are painted and indigo buntings.

Who was the first human to feed birds? A primitive cave dweller, let's call him Unk, probably tossed some scraps of woolly mammoth to an equally primitive bird perched nearby. The bird came closer. Unk tossed more scraps. The bird came closer still. Then Unk probably killed the bird and ate it. Unk's neighbor Oog took note and scratched a note on his cave wall To-Do list to pick up some mammoth scraps next time he went out hunting. Now, I'm not exactly sure that this is how it happened—their names might have been different—but the point is we humans have been feeding birds ever since. Except that now we don't eat them. And our names are nicer than Unk and Oog.

Why Feed Birds?

We feed birds because we like them. And because we like them, we want to see them better—to bring them up close to where we spend most of our time. Whether we're sitting at the kitchen table or outside in a lawn chair, it enriches our lives to have birds there with us.

Perhaps a better question is *Why NOT feed birds?* It's so easy to offer birds the things they need that we really have no excuse not to do it.

It's true that not everyone likes birds enough to want to feed them, however, and there are some reasons not to attract birds. Disease (more about this in Chapter 7), noise (have you ever heard a roosting flock of 10,000 starlings?), mess (bird poop, seed hulls), and the other critters our feeders and food can attract (squirrels, mice, raccoons, bears). Still, when done properly, bird feeding is safe, fun, and enjoyable.

What Birds Need

Birds are found nearly everywhere in the world, from the hottest, most arid desert to the frozen tundra of the Arctic Circle; from the South Pole to downtown Chicago, Los Angeles, and New York. Not every bird can be found everywhere, because birds have specialized habitat requirements. There are no snowy owls in your rosebushes in June in Virginia because snowy owls eat lemmings and small rodents that are found on the aforementioned Arctic tundra. There are no black-chinned hummingbirds at your sunflower-seed feeder in Colorado in January because most hummingbirds consume plant nectar and small flying insects, neither of which is normally available in your backyard in winter. You probably have American goldfinches in your rosebushes in June, and those black-chinned hummingbirds will be back in spring when the nectar starts flowing in the flowers and the insects start hatching in Colorado. There are exceptions to these rules, of course (birds don't read the field guides to figure out their lives, after all), so don't freak out if there *is* a snowy owl in your rosebushes in Virginia. It *could* happen. Or you might just be hallucinating.

One thing we can place our trust in is the list of four basic things that birds need: food, water, shelter, and a place to nest. Not all bird species need all of these things equally, of course. And I hear you screaming for some pertinent examples. Brown-headed cowbirds don't actually nest, or even build their own nests. Instead, over the millennia, their lifestyle of following roaming herds of bison or cattle meant that they had no time to devote to nest building, incubation, or offspring rearing. So they simply deposit their eggs in the nests of other birds and move on,

THESE EASTERN BLUEBIRDS are eating pokeberries. Bluebirds, like other thrushes, eat fruits and berries in addition to insects.

letting the owners of the nests deal with the eggs and young cowbirds.

Many birds don't need water for bathing, and others may not need water for drinking. Hummingbirds rarely drink water because they get plenty of liquid from nectar in flowers and at bird feeders. Wild turkeys and other upland game birds do not use water for bathing. Instead, they use loose soil to take a "dust bath." This has the same useful effect as water bathing. The dust helps discourage feather parasites, which can degrade the ability of a bird's feathers to provide thermal protection and the necessary lift for flying.

By offering the birds around you access to the things they need, you will make your property more attractive to them. Over time, you will attract and enjoy more birds, and that's the point after all, isn't it?

Let's take a closer look at each of these four necessities.

FOOD

Like all other living things, birds need food. When food is abundant, birds appear on the scene to take advantage of it. Perhaps you have seen a flock of American robins in your yard on the first warm, sunny day of spring, pulling earthworm after earthworm out of the recently thawed soil. Or perhaps you've seen a fruiting tree covered in cedar waxwings feasting on the ripe berries.

When food is scarce, birds go elsewhere to find it. This is why we have a mass exodus of certain bird species each fall, heading south in migration, to where their food is still available. This could mean just a few dozen miles, as in the case of our three bluebird species, which move just far enough to find open grassland for foraging. Or it could be the hummingbird at your feeder that will fly thousands of miles to Central or South America where flowers are still blooming and producing sweet nectar.

Not all of our backyard birds move with the seasons. Some species, such as the northern cardinal in the East and the Steller's jay in the West, are year-round residents in their respective ranges. As long as there is ample food available in the habitat within and surrounding their territory, they will stay. But if a food shortage occurs, they will move elsewhere to find sustenance.

There is no single strategy that birds use to get the food they need to survive. Some birds switch their diet instead of migrating to find food. Many species that eat insects during the spring and summer switch over to seeds and fruits from late fall through early spring. Examples of diet switchers include the bluebirds, which consume a much

HUMMINGBIRDS, *like this young male ruby-throated, drink nectar from tubular flowers. This is a cardinal flower.*

higher percentage of plant matter in winter; yellow-rumped warblers, which switch to the fatty berries of wax myrtle plants to survive the insectless winter days; and American robins, which give up the fat, juicy earthworms of summer in favor of a winter diet of fruits and berries.

In the upcoming chapters we'll look at specific ways you can attract birds by offering them things they want to eat. This breaks down into two fairly broad categories: natural sources of food from plants and proper habitat; and "artificial" sources of food in the form of seed, fruit, nectar, and so on at our bird feeders. You'll find tables with recommendations for feeding birds what they want the way they want it on pages 27, 55, and 77.

WATER

Nearly all birds need water in some form or another for drinking, bathing, thermoregulation, and to help with digestion. We humans can relate to the birds' need for drinking water to keep us hydrated and to help with food digestion—just imagine trying to digest an entire mouthful of sunflower seeds with nothing to wash them down with. Gack!

Birds' water requirements for bathing and thermoregulation are a

A MALE EASTERN BLUEBIRD enjoys a bath while a male American goldfinch waits his turn.

bit more complex. Birds bathe to keep their feathers in top condition, and that's a nearly constant job. Dirty feathers not only look ratty; they hinder a bird's flying ability, and they may not provide the necessary insulation against the elements. So birds bathe regularly and preen often—they constantly seem to be messing with and adjusting their feathers.

Naturally occurring water, such as in streams, lakes, puddles, and even the raindrops that collect on leaves, is the most common source of water for birds. Places where a bird can wade into shallow water are the most attractive to them. Where only deep water is available, as in a reservoir, birds can still access the wet stuff by dipping down in flight to skim the water's surface. Among the birds that do this regularly are the swifts and swallows, which have weak feet, short legs, and live most of their days on the wing anyway. A flying drink and in-flight splashy bath seem to suit them just fine.

Where water is not available, such as in arid climates, birds use dust as a water substitute. Many of our desert species take regular dust baths in a convenient patch of loose soil, shifting their wings and tail feathers around and vibrating their body to completely coat themselves. This behavior helps remove excess oil on the feathers and, more importantly, discourages feather mites and other external parasites. Afterward, birds shake and preen off excess dust. Thrashers, sparrows, towhees, and many other backyard species will dust bathe in summer, even when there is water available nearby. It's part of keeping those all-important feathers clean and healthy.

Backyard bird watchers have a wider variety of birdbaths to choose from than they did two decades ago. Gone are the days when the only option was a ceramic or cement bowl on a pedestal. These may look good as lawn décor, but they don't really serve the birds' needs too well. The most attractive way to offer water to birds is in a low-to-the-ground shallow vessel in which the water is circulated. I'll share all the best birdbath secrets in Chapter 3.

SHELTER

One of the most commonly asked questions I hear as a "professional" bird watcher is *Where do birds go at night?* A close second is *What do birds do when it's cold and icy (or violently raining, or the wind is howling)?* The answer is they find shelter. Although birds are better adapted to withstand the elements on a daily basis than we humans are, when really extreme weather hits, birds need to get out of it, just like we do.

But it's not only weather that birds need shelter against. They need to be able to hide from predators and rivals too. Shelter is a constant element in a bird's survival strategy. When we moved in to our farmhouse in southeastern Ohio, we inherited a huge lawn that ran from our house on all sides to the distant woodland edge. We put up bird feeders but got no visitors until we created some islands of shelter to make the woodland birds feel safe. They did not want to cross the vast expanse of open habitat. What if, when a bird got halfway across, a Cooper's hawk appeared hot on its tail? There would be nowhere to hide. Even the grass was too short to offer any kind of useful shelter. Eventually, we transformed our yard into a much more bird-friendly place, but it took some time, some elbow grease, and a bit of trial and error. I'll share some specific examples in Chapter 4.

Now back to those frequently asked questions . . .

Birds seek shelter at night too. Nighttime shelter spots are referred to as roosts. Birds seek a roost where they can rest peacefully, hidden

SHRUBS, BRUSH, AND VINY TANGLES *offer excellent shelter from both predators and harsh weather.*

from the view of predators. This may be in the thick branches of an evergreen or deep in a tangle of thorny raspberry canes. As with bird feeding, there are natural ways to offer birds shelter based on how we plan and manage the habitat in our backyards. We can also offer things like roost boxes, roost shelves, and nest boxes. Cavity-nesting birds such as chickadees, titmice, nuthatches, bluebirds, some swallows, and many woodpeckers will spend the night in a natural roost hole in a tree or in a nest box provided by a thoughtful human landlord.

When extreme weather hits, birds choose shelter spots that help them avoid the effects. In the heat of a desert afternoon, a cactus wren may hole up in the shade of a saguaro cactus. The shade helps keep the bird cool, and by resting, the wren conserves energy it will need for foraging later on when the sun drops and the ambient temperature cools down. During Hurricane Katrina along the Gulf of Mexico, bird watchers reported all kinds of birds hunkering down along the foundations of their houses, where they were protected from the devastating winds. Here in Ohio, a winter ice storm will send all of our bluebirds into our largest nest boxes, where as many as a dozen adults will shelter, sharing body heat all night long until the storm passes and it's safe to leave.

A PLACE TO NEST

Finding a safe place to nest is part of a bird's instinctual imperative. If it cannot find a suitable, safe nesting site, it will not reproduce. If it does not reproduce, its genes will not be passed on to the next generation in the form of viable offspring. And since most of our smaller birds, such as the songbirds, live for just a few years—and most birds don't even make it that far—it does not take long for nesting failure to affect the health of a species' population.

The particular nesting-habitat requirements of certain species can doom it to failure when that habitat type is hard to find. The Kirtland's warbler, for example, nests only in jack pine forests of a certain age—and nowhere else. Fortunately, most of our backyard birds are fairly adaptable and can nest in a variety of situations across multiple habitat types. The ubiquitous song sparrow requires thick, low shrubs for its nests, along with a source of long grass nearby for nest building. The Henslow's sparrow, by contrast, requires open grassland of a certain age with very few shrubs or saplings. This difference in nesting-habitat requirements demonstrates why song sparrows are common and widespread while Henslow's sparrows are so uncommon they get the rare bird alerts going wherever they are found.

In our backyards, providing a diversity of plants—from weeds and grasses to tall, old trees—is the very best thing we can do for birds. It's not a given that if you plant a stand of Virginia pines you'll get pine grosbeaks or pine warblers nesting in them or crossbills coming in for the seed-filled cones. But it is very likely that these same trees, starting when they are just a few feet tall, will provide habitat to a huge variety of birds, from warblers to hawks and owls.

Simply by planning our landscaping with the birds in mind—including the four basic things birds need—we can make our space naturally attractive to these creatures we enjoy so much.

Chapter 2 Bird-feeding Basics

PSSST! HEY! Let me fill you in on a little secret. Birds don't need our bird feeders and all the things we feed them. We feed birds because we like to feed birds. The birds don't really need us in order to survive. They have done just fine for millions of years without our help, and they continue to do so today.

If you believe all the bird-feeding literature and marketing from the companies that make bird feeders and package birdseed, you'd think that our feeding efforts are all that's standing between our beloved backyard birds and the great hereafter. It is true that bird feeding has helped some species thrive and expand their ranges—sometimes for better, or in the case of non-native species like the house sparrow and European starling, sometimes for worse. And it's true that in extremely harsh weather, our backyard offerings may help a few individual birds survive more easily than if there were no feeders, water, or nest boxes. Black-capped chickadees, studies have shown, survive at marginally higher rates if they have regular access to seed at bird feeders during harsh winter weather. Still, it's important to remember that, because we are feeding birds for our own enjoyment, we owe it to the birds to do it right.

In this chapter I share some ideas for getting the most out of your bird-feeding efforts—a good birdy return on your "seedy" investment. And we'll look at how to incorporate some best bird-feeding practices.

Natural Bird Feeding

How would you like to feed birds in the very best way possible—in a way that is all natural, environmentally sustainable, inexpensive, and easy to do? Is that something you might be interested in? If so, get out the garden gloves and the garden trowel and leave the bird feeders and seed alone for now. The best way to feed birds is to offer them the kinds of foods they would find and consume in nature, and that starts with bird-friendly plants.

Birds eat all manner of plant matter: seeds, berries, fruits, buds, leaves, nectar, and of course the insects that occur on and around plants. Every plant from the shortest lichen to the tallest old-growth tree has something edible to offer birds. But it's hard to start a bird-friendly yard with lichens and old-growth trees.

Birds and plants have evolved together on planet Earth. The plant grows a fruit or seed or produces nectar that attracts a hungry bird. The bird returns the favor by helping the plant reproduce itself. This happens in several different ways, but the two most common are as follows. Method (a): A bird eats a part of a plant containing a seed— let's say it's a blackberry—and digests the fruit and poops out the hard, undigestible seeds. The seeds land with a splat on the ground and, with luck and the help of the bird's natural fertilizer, a new blackberry plant grows on that very spot. Method (b): A hummingbird pokes its bill into a honeysuckle blossom and laps up the sweet nectar deep inside. While it's drinking, the flower's pistils are dabbing pollen on the bird's head and bill. The hummingbird carries this pollen to other stands of honeysuckle, helping the honeysuckle to pollinate and reproduce.

If you haven't already guessed it, plants that birds use for food, shelter, or nesting are called bird-friendly plants. The most successful bird-attracting backyards feature a well-rounded selection of bird-friendly plants in addition to feeders, birdbaths, and nest boxes. Usually, it's the plants that initially catch the attention of a passing bird.

SUMAC FRUIT is an important winter food for birds and other wildlife.

On our ridgetop farm in southeastern Ohio, we've planted small stands of gray birches. These trees are native to North America, but they do not occur in our area naturally. However, they survive well enough to grow about 30 feet tall. The birch family is very bird-friendly. Hungry finches eat the birch buds in the spring. The leaves seem to attract every insect and caterpillar in the book, which pleases the warblers and vireos in spring and summer. In fall, the finches munch on the catkins. And the soft wood of the birch trunks is perfect for passing sapsuckers to drill sap wells. In both spring and fall, I've witnessed countless migrant warblers, vireos, tanagers, orioles, and even cuckoos drop out of the sky and make a beeline for the birches. Clearly they recognize these trees as good places to find food.

LETTING IT GO

Sometimes the easiest way to make a yard more bird-friendly is to leave it alone, literally. Nothing is less appealing to our native backyard birds than a large expanse of perfect lawn. Sure, you may get a few American robins or chipping sparrows or common grackles foraging on a huge lawn, but only if that grass still harbors grubs and worms and insects—which most perfect, chemically enhanced lawns do not. In fact, if you are really into having a perfect lawn and plan to soak it with chemicals and fertilizers to achieve the desired level of perfection, you're doing the equivalent of putting up a big sign that says "Native Birds and Wildlife Go Elsewhere!"

If, however, you're open to letting nature dictate, allow a corner or small section of your yard to grow into its full "weedy" goodness. Then watch the birds come in to take advantage of the food and shelter this patch offers. You will likely get a mix of native and non-native plant species.

NATIVE VERSUS NON-NATIVE

North America is overrun in many places with plants that don't belong here. These non-native invaders come from other parts of the world, often to the detriment of our native plants. The birds and animals that rely on our native plants for food and shelter suffer when the habitat is radically altered by the domineering presence of non-native plants. Plants such as pampas grass from South America and Japanese honeysuckle and kudzu from Asia thrive in North America because the factors that keep them under control in their native lands do not exist here. These exotics may do so well that they completely choke out any other competing plant life. If these plants offer nothing of value to our native birds, the birds have no choice but to move elsewhere.

Before planting any new species in your yard or garden, take an inventory of what you've already got. If you can identify any invasive non-native plants, remove them right away. Your local extension service or native plant society can help you with plant identification as well as with suggestions for wildlife-friendly native plant species to add to your property.

BIRD-FRIENDLY PLANTS OVERVIEW

Nearly all plant life has something to offer birds and wildlife. But some plants are more bird-friendly than others, meaning they meet the essential needs of birds on a variety of levels. Here are some general

BRIGHTLY COLORED TUBULAR FLOWERS, such as these gartenmeister fuchsia blossoms, are highly attractive to hummingbirds.

groupings into which we can lump bird-friendly plants, along with some representative plant genera. Please note that it's always best to use native plant species in your bird gardening. Check the plant species name with a reliable resource before you add it to your yard.

ANNUALS

Annuals are plants that have a one-year life cycle. They sprout from seed, produce flowers, ripen their seeds, and then die. This cycle normally runs from spring through fall—essentially one growing season.

Bird-friendly annuals include amaranthus (*Amaranthus* spp.), coreopsis (*Coreopsis* spp.), cosmos (*Cosmos* spp.), marigolds (*Tegetes* spp.), sunflowers (*Helianthus* spp.), and zinnias (*Zinnia* spp.).

PERENNIALS

Perennials are plants that live for more than two years. They bloom and grow for a season, and then die back. The following growing season, they re-emerge from their root stock, rather than regerminating from seed as annual plants do.

Bird-friendly perennials include asters (*Symphyotrichum* spp.), black-eyed Susans (*Rudbeckia* spp.), goldenrods (*Solidago* spp.), coneflower (*Echinacea* sp.), and grasses such as little bluestem (*Schizachyrium* sp.).

SHRUBS

Shrubs are a very general category of broad-leaved plants that have small, tightly grouped branches and thick foliage. They are basically short, leafy trees. Shrubs are excellent sources of shelter and nesting sites, as well as foraging sites, for birds.

Shrubs that are very attractive to birds include sumacs (*Rhus* spp.), elderberries (*Sambucus* spp.), viburnums (*Viburnum* spp.), and boxwoods (*Buxus* spp.).

GARDENS AND WEEDY PATCHES left standing in winter offer a source of seed to sparrows, finches, and other seed-eating birds.

SMALL TREES

Small trees are differentiated from shrubs by their form and growth pattern. Shrubs have multiple branches growing up from the soil. Small trees tend to have a single trunk which then divides into branches and then foliage at some height above the soil. While they may not offer the shelter that thickly vegetated shrubs do, small trees are excellent sources of food for foraging birds.

Bird-friendly small trees include hollies (*Ilex* spp.), serviceberry (*Amelanchier* spp.), and dogwoods (*Cornus* spp.).

FRUITING TREES AND SHRUBS

Fruits produced by plants come in a variety of forms. There's the stereotypical fruit, such as an apple or cherry—colorful, edible flesh surrounding a seed or seeds. But did you know that the samaras (seeds that look like helicopter rotors) of maple trees, the acorns of oaks, and the walnut are also considered fruits? It's true. I don't want to get too deep into proper application of botanical terminology. Let's just say that the most bird-friendly trees and shrubs are the ones that not only provide some sort of shelter and protected site for nesting but also offer the birds something to eat in the way of fruits, nuts, berries, sap, tender buds, or the insects and other prey items that may live on or in them.

Bird-friendly fruiting trees and shrubs include blueberries (*Vaccinium* spp.), cherries (*Prunus* spp.), crab apples (*Malus* spp.), hawthorns (*Crataegus* spp.), mountain ashes (*Sorbus* spp.), spicebush (*Lindera benzoin*), sassafras (*Sassafras albidum*), and black gum (*Nyssa sylvatica*).

These groupings and the species listed under each are a small fraction of the bird-friendly plant options available to you. North America is a huge continent with a range of ecoregions and growing zones. The best bird-friendly plants for your region, climate, soil, and bird-habitat plans will be very different from those of your friend who lives on the opposite side of the continent. For this reason, it's important that you get expert advice specific to your region in order to enjoy maximum bird-attracting success.

There is a table of bird-friendly plants on page 55. This table, along with the basic bird-friendly landscape plan, is a good place to start when you're ready to make your yard more bird-friendly.

CHEMICAL FREE

There's one other bit of advice I'd like to share with you as you plan your bird-friendly habitat. If you can create and maintain your property without resorting to the use of chemical pesticides and herbicides, you'll be doing the birds and the rest of the planet a favor. It's so easy to give in to the hype about having the perfect, weed-free lawn or the biggest, ripest tomatoes or blemish-free apples. Hundreds of millions of dollars are spent each year to convince us that we can achieve better living through chemistry. In the backyard and garden, as far as the birds are concerned, all-natural is the way to go. I've seen enough sick, dying, and dead birds to know that the quest for the perfect lawn has a price. Natural habitats are inherently rough around the edges, so it's perfectly fine for your own bird habitat to look that way too.

Traditional Bird Feeding

Take a look at the shape and size of a bird's bill and you can get a general idea of what that bird eats. That cone-shaped honker on the northern cardinal is made for crushing the hard outer casings of seeds. The chisel-shaped bill of the white-breasted nuthatch is perfect for—yes—prying open seeds and nuts. The tweezerlike bills of our three bluebird species and their relatives in the thrush family are just what is needed to snap tight on a wriggling insect, worm, or grub.

Just as there is no one-size-fits-all bird bill, there also is no one food you can offer in your backyard to attract all birds. Birds' food preferences, like their bills, can differ greatly.

Okay, if you hold me up against the wall and press a suet cake to my forehead, I'll pick the one bird food that is the best if you can offer only one. Black-oil sunflower seed. There! Are you happy now?

Thirty years ago when I was first starting to feed birds, the staple food offered was striped sunflower seed, the hulls of which are gray or black, striped with white. A close second in popularity was some really bad mixed seed that was sold in every grocery store. Then in the early 1980s black-oil sunflower seed came onto the scene. This all-black-hulled seed was formerly known as a source of sunflower oil, extracted by pressing. Its thinner outer shell (or husk) is much easier for birds to open, and the seed kernel inside is comparatively larger than those of the striped sunflower varieties. Once its use as a bird food was discovered, this became the primary channel for the sale and distribution of black-oil sunflower seed.

In the years since it came onto the market, black-oil sunflower seed has become the most widely used bird food in North America. It's so broadly popular with birds and bird watchers that it might be considered (with apologies to our vegetarian friends out there) the hamburger of the bird world.

If forced to choose one bird feeder above all others, I'd have no trouble picking the hopper feeder. Hopper feeders are easy to operate, they protect seed from the weather, and they tend to hold large volumes of food, which they dole out slowly, usually with the help of gravity. Best of all, a lot of birds will use a hopper feeder.

Yes, you can fill a hopper feeder with black-oil sunflower seed. The two go together like toast and jelly. Many backyard bird watchers put up a hopper feeder, fill it with sunflower seed, and that's as far as they go with bird feeding. There's nothing wrong with that, really, though it might get a tad boring.

FEEDER TYPES

Let's look at some basic types of bird feeders. Here's a visualization exercise for you: Get a 50-pound bag of sunflower seed (remember, black-oil sunflower is best). Dump it on your kitchen floor. Count the individual sunflower seeds. Got the number? Are you sure you counted correctly? That's how many different types of bird feeders are available for you to purchase. It wasn't always thus. Back in the 1970s, you either made your own feeders or you bought one sight-unseen from a catalog. Bird feeding had not yet emerged as a viable commercial channel.

Today there are dozens of companies in North America, and thousands more around the world, making bird feeders and other accessories for the backyard bird watcher. Not all of these feeders are perfect—in fact, some are downright useless. Still, there are some general types of bird feeders that are the old standbys: durable, easy to use for both birds and people, and easy to clean.

Commercially available bird feeders come in four basic types: hopper, tube, platform, and globe. The actual designs can vary widely within each of these categories. But the way the food is delivered to the bird doesn't. I'll deal with specialty feeders in a separate section below.

HOPPER FEEDERS

Hopper feeders come in many different styles, but the stereotypical hopper looks like a little barn. The sides are usually panels of Plexiglas or glass, positioned in a V shape. These sides serve to funnel the seed downward and outward as it is eaten, and also allow you to see how much seed remains. Filling access is usually through a removable or hinged panel on top.

The best hopper feeders can be completely disassembled for cleaning. Hoppers can be pole-mounted, often with a threaded sleeve that screws onto the threaded top of a galvanized pipe. They can also be suspended by heavy rope, wire, or a chain, or they can rest on your deck railing.

A MIX OF FEEDER TYPES AND FOODS will attract the widest variety of birds to your feeding station. Basic feeder types, clockwise from top left: globe feeder, tube feeder, platform feeder (lower right), suet feeder, peanut feeder, hopper feeder (center).

The biggest advantages of hoppers are that they hold a lot of seed, so you don't have to refill them every day, and they're big and bird-friendly. Even a medium-sized hopper feeder can accommodate many birds feeding simultaneously. Shy birds or big birds such as doves, jays, and woodpeckers are able to land and feed from them comfortably. In addition, birds that are reluctant to perch on tube feeders or cling to globe feeders will happily come to a hopper, especially if it has a wide platform base.

You can use any kind of seed in a hopper feeder because of its gravity-feed system. Sunflower seed is a favorite of many hopper-feeder visitors. You can also use seed mixes, but don't offer cheap mixes that contain a lot of milo and cracked corn.

TUBE FEEDERS

Tube feeders are long cylinders with perches at the feeding ports. They are the classic feeders for woodland birds such as chickadees, titmice, woodpeckers, and nuthatches, as well as for goldfinches, siskins, and house finches. All these birds are small, and they can perch comfortably on the short perches most tube feeders have.

Like hopper feeders, tube feeders protect the seed from weather while doling out more as birds eat at the feeder ports. Tube feeders are great for deterring large birds such as blue jays, grackles, blackbirds, and doves. Otherwise these species can be aggressive and keep smaller birds away while they vacuum up all the food. Unfortunately, tube feeders also keep grosbeaks and cardinals away too, because these birds are too big for the feeders' perches. These species more readily visit hopper or platform feeders or eat seed spilled on the ground.

Although tube feeders can be pole-mounted, most come with a hanging chain or loop of wire so they can be suspended above the ground. Tube feeders work best when filled with black-oil sunflower seed, sunflower hearts, peanuts (out of the shell), or safflower seed. You can also use special finch mixes. These seed mixes (often called no-waste mixes) are intended for birds that use tube feeders. Cheap mixes that contain a lot of milo and cracked corn are better used for ground-feeding birds.

When you're looking at tube feeders, make sure the seed you're planning to put in them will fit through the holes at the feeding ports. Most tube feeders have big holes that will let sunflower seed through, but others are made especially for tiny Nyjer (also called thistle or niger) seed.

PLATFORM FEEDERS

A platform feeder caters to ground-feeding birds such as doves, towhees, and other sparrows, as well as to larger birds such as grosbeaks and jays. The name says it all: a platform feeder is just that—a platform. It's been only recently that feeder manufacturers started making and marketing platform feeders. Perhaps this was because this style of feeder is simple to make. Just place a large flat object (usually a hunk of plywood) on a tree stump, cinder block, or birdbath pedestal, and you've got a platform feeder.

The advantages of a platform feeder are that it's easy to fill, the birds can find the seed easily, and there's nothing blocking your sight lines. The disadvantages are that platform feeders can lose their seed in high winds or snow, can be dominated by squirrels or large birds, and can be a health hazard if not regularly cleaned. The proximity of birds' droppings to their food can make platform feeders a liability where feeder hygiene is concerned. As gross as it may sound, you'll need to clean the bird poop and seed hulls off your platform feeder (and all of your other feeders too) about once a week. This isn't as hard as, say, washing your car, but from a health standpoint, it's far more important.

To clean the feeder, give it a blast with the hose and scrub it with some hot, bleachy water (1 cup bleach per 1 gallon of H_2O). Let it dry and then refill it.

Today's manufactured platform feeders often have wire mesh bottoms to allow water to drain away quickly. They are designed to be taken apart for easy cleaning and often come with a variety of mounting options, primarily hanging or pole-mounting.

If you want to build your own platform feeder, you can find many different plans on the Internet. Two features that will give your platform feeder maximum utility are a wire mesh floor (for drainage and cleaning) and a short (1- to 2-inch) lip around the edges to keep seed in place.

The platform feeder is the most basic feeder style. It can be used with any food type, and virtually all feeder visitors will use it. For these reasons, a platform feeder is a very versatile part of any feeding operation.

GLOBE, OR SATELLITE, FEEDERS

If you want to cater only to small birds such as chickadees, titmice, nuthatches, goldfinches, and siskins, pick a globe feeder, sometimes called a satellite feeder. It looks like a flying saucer or satellite and is suspended from a wire so it spins when a bird lands on it.

If you're tired of watching large birds hog all the food, try a globe feeder. Birds must approach from the bottom and cling vertically or even upside down to feed. Some globe feeders have a domed baffle on top to keep squirrels out too. In areas where house finches hog the food, globe feeders make it possible for smaller birds to eat.

FEEDER-BUYING ADVICE

Here are some things to consider when purchasing bird feeders for your backyard.

There are many feeder styles on the market, but any feeder you buy should be easy to fill, empty, and clean. Beware of feeders that require you to use a funnel to fill them, because you may tire of lugging a funnel out every time you have to replenish the seed.

Wooden parts of hopper feeders should be made of weather-resistant cedar or stained or painted to protect against moisture. Plastic feeders should be reinforced with metal around the feeding ports to ward off chewing squirrels. Perches should be metal or replaceable dowels for the same "chewy" reason. Because you may be using the same bird feeder for a decade or more, it pays to buy the sturdiest and most easily maintained one you can. Avoid buying feeders that are little more than decorative, a recent trend in feeder design. These may have sacrificed usability for design appeal. They'll look great in your yard, but the birds may never use them.

With tube feeders, look at the bottom port. Is there dead space beneath it where seed can collect because the birds can't reach it? This seed will get icky and moldy—a waste of food and a potential health hazard for the birds. Well-designed tube feeders have parts that solve this problem.

Can you take the feeder apart to scrub and clean it? If it looks like you'll need fancy bottle brushes or special tools to clean it, select one of simpler design.

Beware of really cheap feeders. Not all of the $5 to $10 models available are going to last for more than one feeding season. Remember, these things are going to be filled with seed and hung out in the weather. Look for durable construction if you want to get your money's worth.

SPECIALTY FEEDERS

Suet. Nectar. Peanuts. Fruit. Jelly. Mealworms. Each of these is specialty food that many bird watchers offer to their feathered clientele. Each one also has its own specific method of delivery to the birds. I'll discuss the specific feeders to use with each type of food in the next section.

BIRD-FOOD TYPES

If you really want to be successful at feeding birds (and who doesn't?), this section is worth reading. The most basic attempts at bird feeding can succeed or fail based solely on what food you offer. If you throw out your leftover bread crusts or Pop-Tart corners, you'll get birds, but they'll probably be European starlings and house sparrows, two non-native species that make their living on human leavings. Boooring!

Here are the top 10 foods to offer birds in your backyard. Let me make one caveat here: your bird-feeding mileage may vary when offering these foods. For example, if you live in the hot, arid desert of the Southwest, suet is not really an option. It will melt before you get it in the feeder. Similarly, if you live in New England, you won't get a lot of action at your hummingbird feeder from October to early April. There just aren't any hummingbirds around. So take my advice, but bend it to fit your geographic region, your surrounding habitat, your own backyard, and your personal preferences.

The following 10 foods are extremely popular with backyard birds all across North America. If your favorite bird food is not on this list, please let me know. After all, I am not omniscient. I'm just a guy, living in Ohio, who likes to feed birds.

BASIC SEED TYPES, top row, left to right: peanuts (unshelled), white-striped sunflower seed, safflower seed. Middle row: mixed seed, cracked corn. Bottom row: sunflower hearts, black-oil sunflower seed, millet.

1. BLACK-OIL SUNFLOWER SEED. This is the hamburger of the bird world. Almost any bird that will visit a bird feeder will eat black-oil sunflower seed. Birds that can't crack the seeds themselves will scour the ground under the feeders, picking up bits and pieces. Why do birds prefer it? The outer shell of a black-oil sunflower seed is thin and easy to crack. The kernel inside is larger than the kernel inside a white- or gray-striped sunflower seed, so birds get more food per seed from black-oil. This last fact also makes black-oil a better value for you, the seed buyer. Striped sunflower seed is still fine (evening grosbeaks seem to prefer it slightly), but black-oil is better.

THIS WIRE-MESH FEEDER is designed for black-oil sunflower seed. Here a tufted titmouse (left), a white-breasted nuthatch (right), and a winter-plumaged American goldfinch (bottom) stop by for a bite.

2. PEANUTS. Peanuts (removed from the shell) have been a staple of bird feeding in Europe for decades. Yet despite the position of the United States as the fourth most productive grower of peanuts in the world, feeding peanuts to birds did not catch on here until the mid-1990s. A variety of birds, including jays, woodpeckers, chickadees, titmice, nuthatches, wrens, and even bluebirds and warblers, eat peanuts; roasted peanuts seem most popular.

You can scatter peanuts on a platform feeder, but many people prefer to control the outlay of this somewhat expensive food by using mesh onion bags or cylindrical wire feeders designed specifically for peanuts. Birds can peck off small bits at a time but cannot carry off whole peanuts as easily.

One important note about peanuts: Always dispose of moldy or green nuts in a plastic bag in the trash. Moldy peanuts can be a health hazard for birds.

3. SUET. Most humans don't want a lot of fat in their diet, but for birds in winter, fat is an excellent source of energy. Suet is, simply, fat. More specifically, it's the fat that forms around the kidneys of beef cattle. Butchers remove this stuff, and back when every neighborhood had a butcher shop, they used to give it away to bird watchers. Then grocery stores got smart and started *selling* suet. You've probably seen it—large chunks of white fat wrapped in plastic in the meat case.

Birds love suet, and it is especially valuable to insect-eating species during the winter, when insects are scarce or absent

PEANUTS *are a great way to attract woodpeckers. This is a male northern flicker. Note the black mustache, which females lack.*

from much of the continent. Woodpeckers, bluebirds, warblers, chickadees, titmice, nuthatches, creepers, wrens, wrentits, jays, thrashers, mockingbirds, and even sparrows and towhees are all big fans of suet.

There are two other ways to offer suet to your birds. One way is to make your own suet dough. (See the recipe on page 84.) This starts with melting lard. That is, melt it down to liquid, add corn meal and rolled oats, and then allow it to harden. This is best accomplished in a microwave. Suet dough lasts longer in hot weather, and while it's melted, you can add other ingredients to it (see "Homemade Bird Treats," #10, below).

The other way is to purchase commercially made suet cakes at your local wild bird supply store. Suet cakes are small, preformed pieces of suet, sometimes containing other ingredients. Their main advantage is convenience: remove the packaging and slip the cake into a suet feeder.

So what is a suet feeder? It's a wire-mesh enclosure that allows birds to peck off small pieces of suet. Most suet feeders are designed with a removable lid through which you insert the suet. The feeder hangs from a chain, and birds cling to it while feeding. Some suet feeders are designed to exclude certain suet-hogging species, such as European starlings. They accomplish

A MALE HAIRY
WOODPECKER *visits
a suet feeder.*

this by forcing birds to cling upside down, which woodpeckers and other birds can do, but starlings have difficulty doing. Some suet feeders exclude large birds by placing the dough out of reach inside a cage of wooden dowels. Does this all sound too complicated? No problem—just shove a hunk of unrendered suet into an old mesh onion bag and hang it up outside.

4. GOOD MIXED SEED. Is there such a thing as *bad* mixed seed? Unfortunately, yes. Bad mixed seed has lots of filler in it—junk seeds that most birds won't eat. Bad mixed seed can include dyed seed meant for pet birds, wheat, and some forms of red milo that only birds in the desert Southwest seem to eat. Good mixed seed has a large amount of sunflower seed, cracked corn, white proso millet, and perhaps some peanut bits. The really cheap bags of mixed seed sold at grocery and discount stores can contain the least useful seeds. Buying mixed seed from a specialty bird store or a hardware/feed-store operation is a smart way to go. You can even buy the ingredients separately and create your own specialty mix.

   A wide variety of ground-feeding birds, such as pigeons, doves, quail, sparrows, juncos, towhees, thrashers, blackbirds, and buntings, will scarf up mixed seed. Offer mixed seed on a low platform feeder or scatter it on the ground. In wet weather, scatter only as much seed as the birds will clean up in a day. Wet seed can get moldy and may cause health problems for birds. During snowy or icy weather, our feeder birds really appreciate a few handfuls of mixed seed tossed on the ground beneath our evergreens and thick shrubs. With such protection, the seed doesn't get covered up by the snow.

5. NYJER, OR THISTLE, SEED. Though it can be expensive, Nyjer, or thistle, seed is eagerly consumed by all the small finches—goldfinches, house, purple, and Cassin's finches, pine siskins, and redpolls, as well as the various rosy-finches of the western mountains.

   Nyjer seeds are small and dark. They can't be offered in just any old hopper or tube feeder. You need to feed Nyjer in a thistle feeder. The two most commonly used types are a tube feeder with small thistle-seed-sized holes, and a thistle sock. A thistle sock is a fine-mesh synthetic bag. Small finches can cling to it and pull seeds out through the mesh.

6. SAFFLOWER. Many birds eat this white, thin-shelled, conical seed, which is reputed to be the favorite food of the northern cardinal. Some people claim that squirrels and blackbirds do not eat safflower seed as readily as other seeds, though I've seen both eating safflower. Feed safflower in any feeder that can accommodate sunflower seed. Avoid feeding safflower on the ground in wet weather; it can quickly become soggy and inedible. You can buy safflower in bulk at seed and feed stores.

7. CRACKED CORN. Sparrows, blackbirds, cardinals, jays, doves, quail, and squirrels are just a few of the creatures you can expect at your feeders if you feed cracked corn. Depending on where you live, you may also get turkeys, deer, elk, moose, and other mammals. Fed in moderation, cracked corn will attract almost any feeder species. But therein lies a conundrum: cracked corn can also attract some less-welcome feeder visitors, including large flocks of crows, blackbirds, pigeons, doves, house sparrows, and—bane of many backyard bird watchers—squirrels.

   Squirrels love corn above almost all other food. They will chew a hole right through a wall to get to corn. I know this firsthand. Some feeder operators use this food only to lure squirrels away from their bird feeders. I discuss ways to deal with squirrels in Chapter 7.

   Whole corn that is still on the cob is not a good bird food because the kernels are too big and hard for most small birds to digest. Cracked corn, broken up into smaller, more manageable bits, is ideal for birds. Offer cracked corn on a low platform or scattered on the ground.

8. MEALWORMS. Imagine how a bluebird or a wren feels when, in the middle of a freezing February day, it sees a dish of wriggling, squirming mealworms! Hallelujah! Live food!

   We once fed mealworms to a pair of nesting bluebirds throughout a summer. They rewarded us with four healthy broods of young bluebirds. Eighteen fledglings in one summer should land our bluebirds in the *Guinness Book of World Records*. Most feeder birds, except goldfinches, will eat mealworms if you offer them. Mealworms are available in bait stores or by mail order. Don't worry, they aren't slimy and gross. In fact, they aren't even worms; they are the larval stage of a beetle (*Tenebrio molitor*), if that makes you feel better. We keep 1,000 mealworms in a tub of

**MANY INSECT-EATING
BIRDS** (tanagers, orioles,
warblers) will visit a feeding
station that offers fruit,
such as oranges.

old-fashioned rolled oats and feed them to the birds in a shallow ceramic dish. The dish has slippery sides so the worms can't crawl out.

It's important to note that we no longer offer mealworms to our birds during the insect-rich summer months, when there's plenty of natural food to eat. Too much protein can stimulate an unhealthy amount of breeding in birds. Breeding is hard enough on our birds without their having to suffer through it extra times—we realized that four broods had been a burden on our bluebirds. Two is normal. Three is exceptional. We now offer mealworms in moderation in winter, and only during the very worst weather. Still, this is one of the foods birds are really drawn to, and mealworms are the best way to feed bluebirds.

9. FRUIT. Humans are supposed to eat at least three servings of fruit every day. Fruit is also an important dietary element for birds, but it can be hard for them to find in many regions in midwinter. Set out grapes, slices of citrus, apple, or banana, and even melon rinds, and watch your birds chow down. If you want to feed raisins, chop them up and soak them in warm water first to soften them a bit. Offering fruit to tanagers and orioles is a traditional spring and summer feeding strategy, but many winter feeder birds will also eat fruit. When we find old, wrinkly grapes in the bottom of the refrigerator, we put them on the platform feeder for the red-bellied woodpeckers to eat.

In many parts of the South and Southwest, halves of citrus fruits are stuck on tree stubs or impaled on fencepost nails to feed birds. I've watched exotic green jays, hooded orioles, golden-fronted woodpeckers, various warblers, and chachalacas all visit the same grapefruit half in a backyard in south Texas. If that isn't a vote for offering fruit, I'm handing in my binoculars.

10. HOMEMADE BIRD TREATS. An extremely simple way to feed birds is to smear some peanut butter on a tree trunk and poke some peanut bits into it. If you don't mind a little kitchen prep, another way is to melt suet in your microwave and pour it into an ice-cube tray. Before it solidifies, add peanut bits, raisins, or apple bits. Put the tray in your freezer to harden. Once it does, you've got cubed bird treats. Easy to make and easy to use!

What's for dinner?

Pheasants, Quail	Cracked corn, millet, milo
Pigeons, Doves	Millet, cracked corn, milo, buckwheat, sunflower, baked goods
Roadrunner	Meat scraps, hamburger, suet
Hummingbirds	Plant nectar, small insects, sugar solution
Woodpeckers	Suet, suet dough, meat scraps, sunflower hearts/seed, cracked corn, peanuts, fruits, sugar solution
Jays	Peanuts, sunflower, suet, suet dough, meat scraps, cracked corn, baked goods
Magpies, Crows, Nutcracker	Meat scraps, suet, suet dough, cracked corn, peanuts, baked goods, table scraps, dog food
Chickadees, Titmice	Peanut kernels, sunflower, suet, suet dough, peanut butter
Nuthatches	Suet, suet dough, sunflower hearts/seed, peanut kernels, peanut butter
Creeper, Wrens	Suet, suet dough, peanut butter, peanut kernels, bread, fruit, millet (wrens)
Kinglets	Suet, suet mixes, mealworms
Bluebirds, Robin, Other Thrushes	Suet, suet dough, mealworms, berries, chopped fruits, soaked raisins, currants, nuts, sunflower hearts
Catbird, Mockingbird, Thrashers	Halved apples, chopped fruits, baked goods, suet, suet dough, nuts, millet (thrashers), soaked raisins, currants, sunflower hearts
Waxwings	Berries, chopped fruits, canned peas, currants, raisins
Warblers	Suet, suet dough, mealworms, fruit bits, baked goods, sugar solution, chopped nuts
Tanagers	Suet, suet dough, fruit, sugar solution, mealworms, baked goods
Towhees, Sparrows, Juncos	Millet, sunflower hearts, black-oil sunflower, cracked corn, suet, suet dough
Cardinal, Pyrrhuloxia, Grosbeaks	Sunflower, safflower, cracked corn, millet, peanuts, fruit, suet dough, mealworms
Blackbirds	Cracked corn, milo, wheat, peanuts, table scraps, baked goods, suet, suet dough
Orioles	Halved oranges, apples, berries, sugar solution, grape jelly, mealworms, suet, suet mixes, soaked raisins, currants
Finches	Nyjer, sunflower hearts, black-oil sunflower, millet, fruits, peanut kernels, suet dough

If these ideas don't hold any appeal, do an Internet search for "homemade bird food" and spend a little time leafing through the 1,000,000-plus results you get. Everybody's got a favorite bird-food recipe!

Bird-feeding Myths

Have you ever noticed how much of what we consider "conventional wisdom" is really wrong and ridiculous? Bird-feeding conventional wisdom is riddled with bad information. But you, my friend, are in luck! I have tried almost everything in bird feeding at least once, and I have made nearly every mistake possible. Why? *So you won't have to!*

Here are some incredibly common bird-feeding myths that I will now debunk for you. Check 'em out.

Myth: *Feeders keep birds from migrating.*
Reality: If this were true, we'd have hummingbirds and orioles clinging to our feeders all winter long. Birds migrate when their natural internal "clocks" urge them to do so. Migration is driven by instinct and external factors such as hours of sunlight and weather, not by the availability of food at feeders. One thing to note is that birds need extra food during migration, so it's nice to keep your feeders stocked in case a hungry migrant plops down in your yard looking for food.

Myth: *Bird feeding is really bad/good for birds.*
Reality: Let's face it, birds did just fine before we decided, a few hundred years ago, to feed them. Birds do not need the food we provide for them. It's a nice compromise between our desire to see birds in our backyards and the birds' willingness to take advantage of our largesse. Birds do not rely solely on our feeders for their survival, and they certainly do not rely on our feeders for necessary nutrients, so it's wrong to say that feeding is "good" for birds. By the same token, when bird feeding is done in a conscientious manner, it is also not bad for birds. Yes, messy feeding stations can harbor disease, and food can sometimes spoil at our feeders, but if these scenarios are avoided, bird feeding is enjoyable for us and attractive to the birds. If you wish to stretch the argument to include whether millions of bird feeders have an impact on bird populations, then yes, we can argue about the negative effects of bird feeding. But let's not do that now. Let's go on to the next myth. . . .

WHEN INSECTS are unavailable, bluebirds shift their diet to fruits and seeds. These eastern bluebirds are eating sunflower hearts during a snowstorm.

Myth: *Birds will starve if you stop feeding in winter.*
Reality: Birds have evolved over the eons as incredibly adaptive, mobile creatures. Unless a bird is sick or debilitated, it can use its wings (or legs) to range far and wide in search of food. Birds that cannot move in search of food are likely doomed to perish anyway, which is part of the natural scheme of things. So when you're going away on vacation for two weeks in the middle of a cold, snowy winter spell, it's nice if you can arrange for a neighbor to keep your feeders filled. Most serious backyard bird watchers wouldn't think of letting their feeders go empty. But if it happens while you're gone, as it has happened to me, realize that your birds will not starve, they will just go somewhere else to find food. Then you'll have to work to lure them back!

Myth: *The mixed seed at the grocery store is bad.*
Reality: I believed this with all my heart until recently, when I saw some decent mixed birdseed for sale at a fancy grocery store. Granted, the stuff at my local chain grocery store is still absolute junk, unfit for rock pigeons. But some seed producers seem to be getting the message that quality seed is worth making. The trick to

telling the junk seed from the better stuff is to read the ingredients. Junk seed has almost no black-oil sunflower, peanut bits, safflower, millet, or sunflower hearts. It has lots of milo, wheat, barley, cracked corn, and upon visual inspection, perhaps some empty hulls, sticks, and other inedibles. The best mixes feature a hearty helping of sunflower seed in some form.

Myth: Birds won't eat milo.

Reality: Years ago in an early issue of *Bird Watcher's Digest,* one of our editorial cartoons stated emphatically that "Real Birds Don't Eat Milo." Readers in the eastern half of North America nodded in agreement, but folks in the Southwest howled their ridicule and protested loudly. Red milo is a staple of western bird feeding, especially in the Southwest, where a variety of quail, doves, towhees, and sparrows readily eat it. In the East and upper Midwest, birds don't seem to eat milo much at all, so any mixed seed with a large percentage of milo will probably go mostly uneaten.

Myth: Blackbirds/squirrels won't eat safflower seed.

Reality: Safflower was once considered by many to be the anti-blackbird and anti-squirrel food. Cardinals seemed to love it, but blackbirds and squirrels did not. That's not really true anymore, but nobody knows why. Many folks who feed safflower report that any bird or mammal that eats sunflower will also eat safflower. Safflower seed is still a nice alternative food to offer—it works in any feeder suitable for sunflower seed, and it can be bought in bulk at feed stores. A blackbird and squirrel deterrent it is not, but then again, what is?

Myth: Only one hummingbird species occurs east of the Rocky Mountains.

Reality: Gone are the days when this statement could be considered true. There are even breeding records for other hummingbird species (mainly the buff-bellied hummingbird) in southern Texas. In winter this statement is even less accurate because there can be as many as 10 different hummingbird species visiting feeders throughout the southeastern states. In addition to our regular eastern breeder, the ruby-throated hummingbird, eastern states now regularly play host to rufous hummingbirds, a hardy species that can breed as far north as Alaska. It is unclear if this is a new phenomenon or if the explosive growth of hummingbird feeding and bird-friendly backyard habitat has made these birds more noticeable. I'm still waiting for the first good vagrant hummer at our feeders. Will it be a rufous? A black-chinned? A Calliope?

Myth: *Red dye in hummer food is bad.*
Reality: We'd like to think we know what is best for the birds we feed, but in a lot of cases we don't. It certainly seems logical that adding food coloring to hummingbird nectar solution might not be good for the birds drinking it, but the fact is, we don't have any scientific proof to that effect. So it's one of those innocent-until-proven-guilty things. And until some scientist does the testing, millions of packages of red-dyed hummingbird nectar will continue to be sold and used. (The purpose of the dye is to attract the attention of a passing hummingbird; the truth is that the red or orange parts of hummingbird feeders do a better job of this.)

Equally bad is the assertion by many of the same companies that produce and sell the pre-fab nectar that we need to add "nutritional supplements" to the nectar. Hummingbirds do not need our help to have a balanced diet. Between flower nectar and catching small insects, these tiny birds have everything they need, food-wise, to be healthy.

Your best option is to make your own hummingbird nectar using regular table sugar and water. No dye. No extra anything. That's being a good bird feeder.

Myth: *Perches on hummer feeders are bad.*
Reality: It started out as anecdotal evidence that grew into a wave of mild hysteria. Hummingbird feeders with perches were killing hummingbirds! How? Well, the hypothesis was that hummers would land on a feeder perch in the early morning and drink a deep slurp of very cold nectar, and this jolt of coldness would cause them to go into torpor, a trancelike state in which body functions slow drastically to conserve energy. Some hummers were found hanging upside down from their perches, while others fell to the ground and were at the mercy of predators. Witnesses reasoned that the hummers did not generate enough body heat while sitting and thus succumbed to the cold.

Removing the perches would force the hummers to hover while feeding, thus generating body heat. Now, before you go out and rip the perches off your feeders, consider that there are lots of reasons why a hummer might behave in this way. The bird could be in a natural state of torpor, which is how hummers survive in extremely cold weather. A hummer that has been stung by a bee or wasp will behave strangely, as will one that is sick or perhaps injured from the fighting that occurs near a busy feeder. In my experience, a feeder with perches allows many hummers to feed at once peacefully. Hummingbirds forced to hover at feeders seem to fight more readily and are more active in defending a feeder. As with red dye, we don't have scientific evidence to prove that feeders with perches are bad for hummingbirds, so until we do, use your own good judgment. As for me, I'm pro-perch.

Myth: **This feeder is 100 percent squirrel-proof!**
Reality: I am sorry, but there's just no way. Here I am setting myself up for angry letters from feeder manufacturers, but it is simply impossible to believe this statement. Oh, yes, you can make a feeder squirrel-proof by placing it in the middle of a treeless lawn with a pole-baffle that would do the Pentagon proud. But nail that same feeder to your deck railing, and watch the squirrels remove the confident smile from your face, along with all the seed in your feeder. Squirrels have the drive to be way more resourceful than any bird-feeder designer. Why? Because a squirrel is working to feed itself and perhaps its offspring, and it will throw itself into the task with all its might every single day. The squirrel thinks of nothing else but the seed inside that feeder and how to get at it. The feeder designer, meanwhile, is thinking about lunch and vacation and next Tuesday's staff meeting and his bowling league. That's why the squirrels win every time.

A Basic Feeding Station

Each feeding station has its own advantages and shortcomings. But that's all part of the challenge and joy of bird feeding: there's always something new to try, to learn, to enjoy.

If you are just starting out, I suggest you start simply, with just a feeder or two. I'd suggest a basic tube or hopper feeder with some black-oil sunflower seed and perhaps a low platform feeder with some good mixed seed.

See how things work. It will take the birds a while—perhaps several weeks or months—to find your feeders, especially if your yard has never had feeders before. Once they do find your feeders, you'll be able to tell, over time, if what you're offering is right. You can then expand your offerings from there.

Beyond the Basics

Before too long, you may want to try something new at your feeding station. After black-oil sunflower and mixed seed, the next logical steps are a peanut feeder and some suet or suet dough/cakes. These feeders and foods can be found at any store that carries a decent array of bird-feeding supplies.

You may also wish to try some new feeder styles. At our farm, we enjoy feeding Carolina wrens and eastern bluebirds in a small plastic feeder that sticks to our kitchen window. We offer suet dough and some mealworms in this feeder. These two species spend most of the spring and summer nesting close to our house, so they are not afraid when they see us through the window. We've developed a special relationship with these birds by offering them specific foods in a feeder meant exclusively for their use.

You'll find this to be true in your bird feeding too. As you watch the birds coming and going, you'll begin to note certain ones as individuals. You'll see that the chickadee with the tiny spot of white on its black crown is the most avid defender of the peanut feeder. The song sparrow that comes to the suet dough first will be waiting when you emerge from the house on a cold winter morning. This is no accident. That bird recognizes you as the Food Lady or Feeder-filler Guy. Isn't that cool?

Way Beyond the Basics

There is almost no limit to what I'll do to connect with my backyard birds. Every time we have eggs for breakfast or use eggs in a recipe, we hand-wash and set aside the shells. Then we bake them in the oven (250 degrees for 30 minutes). We put them in an old jar and crush them into tiny bits with a wooden spoon.

Why? Am I crazy?

Well, yes, but that's not why I do this.

All summer long the barn swallows that nest in our neighbor's hay barn come over to our farm to get eggshell bits. They eat them, and this helps enhance their calcium levels, which evidently helps them produce healthy eggshells of their own. It's also thought that when the barn and tree swallows and the bluebirds, goldfinches, house finches, blue jays, flycatchers, gnatcatchers, tanagers, orioles, and sparrows eat

CRUSHED EGGSHELLS help birds, such as this barn swallow, replenish calcium and other important nutrients.

our eggshells, the tiny sharp fragments aid their digestion by helping grind up hard bits of insects or seeds.

Here are some other crazy things we've fed our birds.

MEAT PILE

We put out freezer-burned meat once or twice a year for the birds and other animals to eat. Of course, we live in the country and we have a large meadow, so we don't get complaints from neighbors about the scavengers we attract to our meat pile. Then there's the smell, which can be a bit off-putting. But we get rewarded with views of vultures, hawks, foxes, coyotes, and other creatures.

MELON RINDS

In summer, after you've eaten that really yummy watermelon, consider leaving the rind out where the birds can find it. Our thrashers and towhees love it when we put out melon leftovers, including the seeds.

MOTH-RIDDEN EDIBLES

Rice, flour, pasta, cereal, pancake mix—all of it seems to attract Indian meal moths at our house. Sometimes this happens before we get to eat much of it ourselves. Rather than just tossing this stuff in the garbage bag, we put it on our compost pile. Last summer, the common yellowthroats that nest near the compost pile must have thought they'd died and gone to buggy heaven.

DEAD GARDEN

Long after our garden has produced its last tomato and hot pepper, we leave it for the birds. Our serious vegetable gardener friends are horrified by this, but they're not here in the winter when the juncos and tree sparrows are picking up seeds in the dead stalks. Or when the eastern phoebe and palm warbler are catching fruit flies that hover around the rotten tomatoes.

Feeder Maintenance and Keeping Things Going

If your bird-feeding set-up is as active as mine is, you'll find yourself doing a fair bit of feeder maintenance. You'll be cleaning feeders and cleaning up around the feeders. You may even have to move or repair the feeders, depending on how heavy your feeder traffic is. And of course, you'll also have to refill your feeders regularly.

FILLING UP

I store our birdseed in our garage in a 50-gallon plastic trash can with a lockable lid. Mice and raccoons have chewed their way into the can over the years, but that was before we got serious about keeping the garage doors closed at night. The storage can holds a 50-pound bag of sunflower seed, plus all the smaller bags of mixed seed, sunflower hearts, and peanuts that are part of our regular feeder offerings. Next to the seed storage can, I have a couple of large buckets that I use to haul seed to the feeders. There are a couple of scoops, a feeder-filling funnel, and some smaller cans. I fill a 5-gallon bucket or two with black-oil sunflower and a smaller bucket halfway with cracked corn and halfway with mixed seed. The peanuts live in their own container. All of this goes into a giant muck bucket, which I haul out to the main feeder station.

After filling the main feeders, I scatter some seed under the pines, under the spruce, and along the weedy edge of the compost pile. This gives the shyer sparrows and towhees a source of seed closer to their preferred habitat.

Once I've filled the yard feeders, I turn my attention to the suet-dough feeders on the back deck and front stoop.

When, during my daily rounds of feeder filling, I notice that the feeders or the ground beneath them are getting really gross, I make plans for a maintenance day. That involves a different bucket.

CLEANING THE FEEDERS

Hundreds of hungry, feeding, bickering birds produce a lot of bird poop. Much of that bird poop falls to the ground with all the discarded seed hulls. Yum! But some of the poop lands on the feeders and even in the food. As responsible landlords, we owe it to the birds to keep our feeders clean and healthy.

The first order of business when cleaning feeders is to get your gear together. I take a bucket of warm bleachy water (9 parts water to 1 part bleach), a scrub brush, a long feeder brush, a putty knife, a chopstick, and some rags. First I knock all the seed and poop and crusted hulls off the feeder. What won't fall off I scrape off with the putty knife. I poke the chopstick into the hard-to-reach places around the feeding ports and in the bottom of tube feeders. Then I give the feeders a good soaking in the bleach water and a scrub with the brush. After that, a few shots with the hose to remove any lingering gunk, and then I leave the feeders out in the sun to dry.

REGULAR CLEANING of feeders helps keep birds healthy and is vital in reducing disease transmission among feeder visitors.

If the feeders have deeply encrusted gunk, I soak them overnight in a big muck bucket.

It's a pretty unpleasant job, but it feels better to have it done than to see sick birds hanging around the yard—birds that may have gotten sick at my dirty, poop-covered feeders.

REPLACING OR REPAIRING FEEDERS

There is a limit to how long a feeder will last. Even the best-built bird feeders will eventually succumb to the ravages of weather, weight, and usage. You'll know when it's time to replace a feeder. Things to watch for include ports that do not restrict the outward flow of seed, lids that are missing or no longer working, and sharp edges jutting out from the feeder.

At our farm, the raccoons used to beat the tar out of our feeders so often that we had to replace them frequently. A new set of raccoon-proof baffles on the feeder poles is helping us limit the damage to almost nothing now.

Read more on dealing with predators in Chapter 7.

Chapter 3 Water for Birds

IN CHAPTER 1 WE LEARNED WHY BIRDS NEED WATER and how they get it. In this chapter we'll look at a variety of ways you can provide water to birds.

Numerous times and in numerous places when I've been out watching birds, I've found a natural watering spot for birds along a stream, lakeshore, or pond. These places all have two things in common: they offer shallow water with good footing, and they are places where a skittish wild bird can feel safe pausing to bathe or drink.

Why are these characteristics important? Let's take a closer look.

A MALE EASTERN TOWHEE bathes in a small ground-level birdbath.

Feeling Safe

A bird that lives its life in the treetops needs to gather its courage to venture to the ground to visit a source of water. Danger is all around a small songbird such as a warbler. It is small enough to be captured, killed, and eaten by almost anything, including opportunistic bird-eaters such as a blue jay or common grackle. It's much more vulnerable to attack by snakes, house cats, and wild mammals such as weasels and raccoons when it is on the ground. A nearby sharp-shinned or Cooper's hawk might just be quick enough to catch it before it can burst into an escape flight. So the place a bird chooses to drop down to a water source, such as a pool along a stream, needs to have open sightlines around it so the bird can detect approaching danger. The place also needs to have nearby cover into which the bird can escape.

Drinking is one thing. A warbler can nip down, scoop up a few bills full of water, tilt its head back to drink it down, and be gone. Bathing is another thing. When a bird bathes fully, it gets most of its feathers soaked. Most songbirds accomplish this not by sitting down in water up to their neck as we humans often do, but by wading into the water up to their belly and ducking down to splash the water over the rest of their body. This makes their bathing a rather splashy, active affair. Wet birds cannot fly as well as dry birds, so they are vulnerable while bathing and immediately afterward, until they dry off. So once fully soaked— and looking fairly bedraggled—a bird will move off a short distance to a safe perch. There, it will shake off the excess water and begin to preen its feathers back into place, cleaned and freshly reconditioned.

When a wild bird finds a reliable and safe bathing and drinking spot and uses it successfully, the spot will become a regular part of the bird's routine. There is just such a site along the perennial stream in the east valley here on our farm. The roots of a giant sycamore sit opposite a

AMERICAN ROBINS *lean forward and splash water through their feathers when bathing.*

nice shallow bowl in the sandstone bank. When the creek is at normal levels, this bowl serves as a natural birdbath. I've seen every common bird in our woods bathing there, in addition to some less common visitors, including winter wren and hermit thrush in winter and worm-eating warbler and rose-breasted grosbeak in spring. I'm also fairly certain I've scared our local barred owl up out of the bathing spot a few times as I approached. The point is this: all these birds have found this bathing site and have made it part of their regular routines.

I wish this awesome natural birdbath were in my backyard. Unfortunately, it's a quarter of a mile down the hill, deep in the woods. Our house and backyard are on a dry ridgetop with no naturally occurring reliable source of water for birds.

We have other natural water sources too. The low spots in our yard and driveway often hold water after a heavy rain or snowmelt. The birds use these while they are available, but these are not reliable sources of water. We also have a few seeping springs around the farm. Many years ago, one of these was dug out to create a watering hole for cattle. The spring continues to produce prodigious amounts of water all year long even though the small enclosure is mostly filled in now. I make a point of digging out a few square feet each spring for the frogs and toads to use. The birds use it too, but like our streamside birdbath, it's too far from the house for us to observe regularly.

If you have a natural water source on your property, one that's easy to watch and enjoy from your favorite vantage point, consider yourself lucky. Most of us have to create this particular piece of paradise in order to add it to our offerings.

How do you do this? We try our best to emulate a really nice natural source here in our yard.

Basic Birdbath

Here's what not to do. Don't run down to your local big-box store and buy a beautiful ceramic birdbath with a deep bowl and a lovely, shiny finish on it for just $11.97. I'm not arguing with the price, mind you. It's the deep bowl and the slick finish. Unless you just want a piece of lawn decoration that will never be used (or pooped on) by a bird, avoid the products that put form over function.

The deep bowl, when filled with water, will be too deep for birds to use safely. Most birds prefer fewer than 2 inches of water for bathing.

The slick bottom of a ceramic (or metal or plastic) birdbath bowl is very unattractive to birds. If they perch on the edge of the bowl and feel the slippery surface, they may never venture any closer to the water. Slick footing makes it difficult to splash around while bathing, and it can make it harder to take off quickly if danger approaches. Both scenarios will make birds feel less safe, which means your birdbath won't become a part of their regular routine.

But all is not lost, Grasshopper. Even the deepest and most slippery birdbath bowls can be changed for the better. The solution is to add a few flat rocks to the middle of the bowl. The best rocks are wide, flat ones that will rest just an inch or so below the water's surface. Add another one that is taller, creating an island in the bowl's middle.

This solution covers the water depth and safe-footing problems, making your formerly unappealing birdbath much more appealing to passing birds.

BUYING A GOOD BIRDBATH

If you are in the market to purchase a birdbath, look for—yes—a wide and shallow bowl made from a material that will give birds' feet a bit of "grip." You can certainly buy one of these at most garden centers and nature stores, but be aware that you do not necessarily need to add the pedestal, which holds the bowl of water 3 or more feet off the ground. I've never had much success with raised birdbaths, perhaps because birds are accustomed to finding water on or near the ground and do not "tune in" to a bath 3½ feet up.

CONCRETE

The classic material for a birdbath is concrete molded into a bowl-like shape. Concrete is heavy, which reduces tipping problems when large birds, mammals, or family pets inevitably use it. Concrete baths can be so heavy that you'll loath tipping the bath out to clean it, something we'll discuss further in a moment. Baths made from concrete or composite materials have the advantage of being durable and even freeze-proof, meaning if the water in your bath freezes in winter, it may not crack the bowl and ruin it. Another factor with concrete baths is the surface texture. Concrete baths generally offer birds good footing when bathing or drinking, but that same rough surface can be a bear to clean once it gets covered in green algae. This is where having a good hose with a blast-force nozzle and a scrub brush comes in.

PLASTIC

Plastic baths can be all right if you place them where they won't tip and augment them with rocks or gravel to give the birds secure footing. They are easier to clean than cement baths, but they cannot withstand freezing. Let a plastic birdbath freeze hard once, and it will probably crack, making it useless. For use in warm climates and during the warmer months, plastic baths work just fine. In summer, we place plastic basins in shady spots around our farm yard. In winter, we dump them out, scrub them, and store them in the garage until spring.

COMPOSITE MATERIAL

The emergence of composite-material birdbaths—more durable than plastic and less unwieldy than concrete—is a welcome trend for backyard bird watchers. Composite materials combine two or more ingredients, such as resin, plastic fiber, wood fiber, and concrete, to enhance strength and durability. Composite material can be molded into any shape, and this is how some of the most attractive baths are now made. By attractive, I mean attractive to both birds and humans. On our farm, we have a couple of composite birdbaths, both of which are molded to look like natural rock or stone. This bit of visual trickery makes these baths much more appealing to birds, which cannot tell, at a glance, that the water in the baths is actually trickling alluringly over fake stones. It looks natural to the birds, which makes them want to visit the water. Such design also makes our backyard look slightly more natural—emulating one of the truly natural water features elsewhere on our farm, far from sight.

When buying a birdbath, consider the following:

Is this something I'm willing to look at for the next several years? The bath shaped like SpongeBob Squarepants is cute, but . . .

Is this bath well constructed? Baths made of thin plastic or from materials that won't hold up in extreme weather might be inexpensive, but you'll need to replace them more often.

Is it easy to fill and clean?

If I were a bird, would I be attracted to this bath? This may seem like a silly question, but thinking like a bird has saved me from making some wasteful purchases at the wild bird store.

WHERE TO PLACE THE BATH

Once you have your spanking new birdbath, you need to figure out where to put it. Start by looking out at your yard or garden from the window where you spend the most time. Look for a nice, level spot—one you can easily see, access, and reach with your garden hose and an outdoor electric cord. Found it? OK. Now go outside and check the site again. If it still meets all of your criteria, you've got a good spot. If not, make the necessary adjustments.

Ideally you've chosen a spot that offers birds easy flying approaches and exits. The spot should have some shade during the day so that direct summer sun does not evaporate all the water too quickly. It should not be beneath a popular overhanging perch, however, or the birds will unwittingly poop into the bath. Cover should be nearby, allowing birds to approach the bath cautiously, preen after bathing, and take instant shelter from predators.

Resist the urge to place the birdbath right next to your window or door. As I mentioned earlier, birds are skittish when bathing. Placing the bath too near a lot of visible human activity will only add to their reluctance to use the bath. I normally place our bath about 15 to 20 feet away from our studio windows. It is on the way to our feeding station but at a safe distance from falling seed hulls and bird droppings. It's shaded by a medium-sized clump of gray birches. Next to the bath, I place a small open brush pile of dead branches. This serves as a way station for birds investigating the bath. Nearly every new species we've had visit the bath has followed this same path: Land in the birches, move to the branches near the bath. Drop down onto the brush pile. Hop close to the bath. Flutter over to the edge of the bath for a drink or a quick dip.

But there's a secret weapon that we use to lure birds to our birdbath.

ADDING MOTION

Birds love water, but they find *moving water* irresistible. There are many ways to add motion to the water in your otherwise motionless birdbath. The easiest way (though not the least expensive) is to purchase a bath with a recirculating pump built into it. Among the many choices available for such a device are the baths that feature a reservoir and a filtered pump. Large models can run for days or even a week without needing to be refilled. There is maintenance involved in keeping not only the basin but the filter and pump clean. But once running, they provide *clean* moving water for your birds. Although there are some solar-powered birdbaths on the market, most of these units require electricity to run the pump.

RECIRCULATING BIRDBATH PUMPS

Here's how a filtered-pump recirculating birdbath works: Water is sucked from the reservoir, filtered by the pump, and pumped up and out into the basin. Over time, all the water in the bath is filtered and recirculated. The motion prevents insect larvae, including mosquitoes, from surviving in the water. Algae will still form in the basin, as with any bath, and you'll need to scrape, scrub, and bleach the surface to keep it from taking over. There's more on cleaning techniques on page 45.

MISTERS AND DRIPPERS

On the other end of the spectrum are the misters and drippers that you connect to your garden hose and place in or above a basic birdbath. You can regulate the drips or spray from the small-diameter connector

YOUR BIRDBATH *may attract some surprise visitors, as ours did when a migrant dickcissel stopped by to drink and bathe.*

hose to minimize the amount of water used, but the one drawback to this method of adding motion is that it still uses a lot of water over time. Most garden centers and wild bird stores sell misters and drippers.

WIGGLERS AND MILK JUGS

Two more water-conserving ways to add motion to your birdbath are easy to implement. One is a do-it-yourself project, the other a recently introduced product. First, the product: the Water Wiggler.

The Water Wiggler lives up to its name: it puts a wiggle in your water—at least for as long as the batteries last. When it's on, the Wiggler uses small wire loops to produce constant ripples of water. Place it in the middle of your shallow bird basin, and it looks like an unobtrusive half-dome. If the price (about $40) feels a bit steep to you, I have two words: *milk jug.*

Get your hands on an empty 2-gallon milk jug and make sure it's completely rinsed clean of any dairy residue. Fill it with water, replace the cap, tie a piece of rope to the jug handle, and suspend it above your birdbath. Use a pin to poke a couple of holes in the bottom of the jug. Ease open the cap on the milk jug until the water starts dripping from the bottom of the jug. Adjust position and flow as necessary. When the jug is empty, yes, you'll need to refill it.

There are hundreds of options for adding motion to a backyard birdbath. If you don't believe me, just take a Google for yourself on the Internet. Or spend a little time at your local wild bird store or well-stocked garden center.

FILLING IT, PLUGGING IN

If you do decide to purchase a birdbath that recirculates the water with a pump, you will need to take this into account when you site your bath. It's acceptable, if not exactly stylish, to run a bright orange extension cord out to the bath from the nearest electrical outlet.

Better yet, bury the electric line inside some conduit to keep the cord safe from lawn mowers, pets, and rodents and to give you one less thing to trip over in the yard. Many birders feel better getting a professional electrician to handle this chore. And while you've got a professional at the house, ask him or her to install a ground fault circuit interrupter (GFCI) for you. A GFCI is a specific type of outlet that switches off when a short is detected. You have seen GFCI outlets in hotel bathrooms, with their "test" and "reset" buttons. It's essential that you use a GFCI to supply power to your outdoor birdbath. The combination of electricity, water, and you creating an accidental bridge between leaking current and the ground is potentially deadly. If you do not already have a GFCI on your outdoor electrical outlets, wait to plug in your birdbath until you can get one installed.

OVER THE TOP

If you're really intent on supplying the birds with a natural-looking water source, you might want to consider putting in a small shallow pond, waterfall, or artificial stream with a recirculating pump. You can do this yourself with or without one of the water-feature kits that are available commercially, or you can hire a professional to do it. If you do hire a landscaper to put in your water feature, make sure he or she understands that you want something that will be attractive to and useful for birds and wildlife. Otherwise you might get a deep hole with no shallow edge and a Greek goddess pouring the water from an urn back into the pool. This will not only scare away birds, but it might also scare away your neighbors.

The term "water feature" may mean two completely different things to you and your local landscaper. Do some research beforehand so you can launch the project with a clear idea of what you want. The birds will appreciate your extra effort.

LARGE WATER FEATURES like this fishpond also attract birds. Make sure to offer a shallow area where birds can comfortably access the water.

MAINTENANCE

Now for the fun part: keeping your birdbath clean. A dirty bath is potentially unhealthy for birds. As stewards of our backyard nature, we owe it to our "customers" to provide them with healthy access to our offerings.

Let's face reality. The second you fill your pristine birdbath with water and step away to admire it, that same bit of clear liquid begins its inevitable and ongoing slide toward algae-clogged oblivion. Bird poop will soil it, insects will lay their eggs in it, seed hulls and leaves will fall into it, and weird stuff will get in there too: common grackles will sometimes dump their nestlings' fecal sacs into a birdbath—or even a backyard swimming pool (bleeech!).

This disturbing trend toward the icky and gross can be easily thwarted. First of all, you should make a habit of dumping out the birdbath basin at least once a week—more often during periods of heavy use. While the bath is empty, attack it with a scrub brush and garden hose. Dump. Clean and scrub. Refill. That will work for most of the time.

Then there are those *other* times.

When your bath basin starts to take on an overall tone of algae green, it's time to take your cleaning to another level. Don't worry. You won't need a pressure suit, an aqualung, or any heavy-duty equipment. You will, however, need some rubber gloves and a cleaning agent that has some algae-killing bleach in it.

Here's how we do it on our farm.

We have a lovely birdbath, called a Bird Spa by brand name. It features a 6-gallon reservoir in the base; a powerful pump and filter, which pushes the water up to burble out across a fake-stone central island; and a wide, shallow basin that's very appealing to birds. The whole thing is made of durable fiberglass. Our birds use it so much that we need to clean it frequently in the spring and summer.

Before the weather gets really warm, a good scrubbing with a light bleach-water solution works just fine to keep things clean. (We use 9 parts water to 1 part bleach for this.) Then we follow the scrubbing with a good rinse to reduce the risk of bleach water being left behind.

When the weather is warmer—from June through September—we need to augment this cleaning technique with some abrasive cleaning product. A powdered abrasive such as Comet and a short-bristled scrub brush really do the trick. The warmer weather encourages algal growth, which appears on the sides and bottom of the basin. Despite the often-propagated myth that you'll doom your birds to certain death if you let your birdbath get covered in algae, the algae itself is not necessarily harmful to birds. But left unchecked, it will make your bath basin a real mess—appealing to neither birds nor you.

Before it gets to that stage, give your basin a good scrubbing out, with either the bleach water, the cleaning agent, or both in succession. Then give the bath a good rinsing with clean water and refill. After the bath has been cleaned, we often see our birds literally lining up to bathe in the clean water!

A dirty birdbath doesn't do anyone any good—least of all the birds. I guess the best advice I have for you is this: if you find it hard to keep up with your birdbath maintenance, it's probably better not to have a birdbath. And what fun is *that*?

WINTER BIRDBATH

Our Bird Spa birdbath is not built to withstand winter temperatures that would freeze the water in it. So when winter hits its stride, we empty the spa and store it in the garage until spring. In its place we put a small concrete bath to which we add an electric heater. The heater plugs into our same GFCI-equipped outside electric outlet. It runs on a thermostat, kicking on anytime the water in which the heater is submerged drops into the low 30s (F). This keeps a small area of water open around the heating unit, allowing birds to drink even on the coldest days of the year. Small birdbath heaters, including ones that run on solar power, can be purchased at most specialty wild bird stores and on the Internet.

Next to our back patio, where our small fish and frog pond is, we use a larger outdoor water heater to keep a portion of the surface ice-free. This heater is designed for use in livestock watering troughs. Such units can be purchased at almost any hardware or feed/seed store that caters to farmers or ranchers.

CLEANING PUMPS AND FILTERS

Most submersible pumps for birdbaths are simple things and easy to rinse out with a hose. Before you mess with the pump and filter, remember to unplug it from the electricity source. Some pumps can be damaged if they continue to pump when removed from water.

Filters normally need only a good hosing off. We sometimes have to pick ours clean of grass bits before hosing it off, especially just after the lawn has been mowed. It's a good idea to have an extra filter or two on hand for your birdbath pump. If the pump is in constant use, you might go through a filter in a year.

NO VISITORS

If you get a nice new bird basin and follow all the instructions above about design, placement, and access and *still* you have no visitors, you can do one of two things: be patient and wait for the birds to find the bath, or move the bath to another site — perhaps nearer to cover, where the birds can feel safer visiting.

Like your feeders, a birdbath is something you provide for yourself as much as for the birds. Birds can find water somewhere nearby—flying ability is a great advantage in this search. So they won't suffer if your yard lacks a functioning water feature. A functioning bird bath, however, is a wonderful way to attract woodland birds, such as warblers, vireos, tanagers, and orioles, that won't regularly visit your feeders.

HOT, DRY SUMMER AFTERNOONS can be a busy time at a water feature. Here, three eastern bluebirds and a male northern cardinal are visiting our large shallow bath. The recirculating water creates noise and motion, alerting the birds to the bath's presence.

Chapter 4 Gimme Shelter

TO MOST PEOPLE, a dead or hollow tree is nothing more than a hazard—something that might topple over unexpectedly and destroy the roof of the house, or worse yet, crush Fluffy the beloved poodle while she's chasing bunnies in the yard. To the discerning eye of the backyard bird watcher, however, a dead tree is a fabulous feature of a bird-friendly yard. An old, dead tree full of woodpecker holes and natural cavities can be a veritable condominium for birds and other creatures that make a backyard more wild and diverse than the typical suburban lawnscape.

There are other bird-friendly features that you might never see featured in a landscaping segment on Martha Stewart's TV show: brush piles, weedy edges, a garden gone to seed and left fallow, messy wood or rock piles, overgrown fencerows. All of these features offer shelter to birds, and shelter, as you may recall, is one of the four crucial elements that birds need to survive.

In this chapter, I'll cover some of these bird-friendly features in detail, give you instructions for adding them to your yard, and even tell you how to explain to your nosy neighbors what it is you're doing.

Planning Your Bird Habitat

Take a look at your yard as it currently is. Do you notice certain parts that the birds use more regularly than others? If so, what are the elements that the birds are using? Do the sparrow flocks shelter in

THIS IMAGE shows two sets of edge habitat: the edge where our lawn meets our grassy meadow and the edge where our meadow meets the nearby woods.

the brambles along the back fence? Did the jays nest in the pines? Are the woodpeckers excavating another nest hole in the old oak tree? Where do the feeder birds go when they are startled? Chances are you are already providing shelter in several ways to your backyard birds.

BRUSH PILES *provide excellent shelter year-round. In snowy weather they also provide a clear patch of ground for bird feeding.*

Birds need shelter from weather and predators every single day and night, all year long. Typically, this comes in the form of thick cover: conifer trees with their dense needles, shrubs with closely growing branches, thick ground cover such as weeds and grasses, cavities in trees, tangles of vines or ivy, and so on. Birds also need places to nest during the breeding season, which for most of them occurs in spring and summer. Some birds, such as rock pigeons and mourning doves, will nest any month of the year if there is enough food and a reliable nest site.

As you look around your yard, do you notice areas that are not used much at all by the birds? Perhaps there's a large expanse of lawn that no one ever uses—you or the birds. Or maybe you have an old flower garden that needs an overhaul. Is there a part of your property that is a real pain to mow and trim? These are ideal candidates for a bird-friendly makeover.

The primary difference between most landscaped backyards and naturally occurring bird habitat is diversity. A suburban backyard, at its least diverse, has lots of lawn, perhaps a few scattered trees, and a shrub or two in some squared-off flower beds with bark mulch covering any bare soil. If you are a bird, unless you are an American robin, common grackle, house sparrow, or song sparrow, there's not much there to attract you.

Now look at a patch of birdy natural habitat. It has dozens of different plant types: trees, shrubs, saplings, vines, grasses, and brambles, plus all kinds of plant matter covering the ground—dead trees, leaves, ferns, mosses, lichens, and many ground-cover plants. In short, it's a rich, jumbled mess of bird habitat and a far cry from what the human eye normally considers to be a well-kept yard or landscape.

This jumble of diversity is what you need to create if you want to attract the maximum variety of birds to your property. It does not need to be messy, necessarily, but neither should it be so tidy that it's less attractive to birds. A happy medium should be your goal.

So how do we achieve that happy medium?

Don't worry—I have a plan!

Consider the two ends of the spectrum for the habitat in your yard. There's probably some area of lawn and, if you're lucky, a few tall, well-established trees. That—literally—is the short and the long of it. Filling in the habitat in between is how we create bird-friendly habitat. But merely throwing any old ground-cover plants, shrubs, fruit trees, and hedgerows into the mix is not going to do it. We need to add the *right* plants to the mix.

IN FALL, the unmown portion of our meadow colors up like the surrounding trees. We leave half of the meadow uncut as shelter and foraging habitat for sparrows, juncos, and finches.

Conventional wisdom might say that you should go to your local garden center or perhaps consult your county, state, or provincial agriculture or soil-conservation office for advice. That's where conventional wisdom can get you into a world of headaches with bad advice. Garden centers—the bad ones, anyway—are in the business to sell you stuff. They may not give a hoot if the plant they sell you is an invasive exotic that will, in a few short years, take over your entire backyard. And we have government policy to thank for the thousands of miles of Russian olive and crown vetch along our highways and the multiflora rose in our woodlands and fields.

Instead, what you need to find is a solid source of advice about bird-friendly plants native to your region. There are, of course, garden centers that specialize in this kind of helpful, accurate, environmentally suitable planting advice. And there are even sources of excellent native plant advice available from our local and regional governments. Unfortunately, that's not the norm.

Every region has a list of recommended bird- and wildlife-friendly plants. If there's not a native plant expert or authority in your immediate area, try searching for one on the Internet.

What's so important about native plants versus just any old plant that's available and will grow in your region's climate and soil? Native plants and native wildlife have evolved over millions of years in harmony. Native birds use native plants, and vice versa. The brown thrasher that eats the wild grapes in fall helps propagate the wild grape when it poops out the grape's seeds after digesting the juicy flesh of the fruit. The fleshy fruit of the grape sustains the thrasher so it can mate and make more thrashers each spring. It's a natural bargain between two living things that helps guarantee that both will send their genetic material into the future.

Enter a non-native plant. On our farm we have a species of pampas grass that is tall and beautiful and horribly invasive. It came into our property from an old country cemetery at the end of our township road. The feathery seed heads of this grass were used in flower bouquets that were placed on graves. The seeds were blown by the wind into the freshly turned soil, and they took. In a big way! That end of the township road is now covered in pampas grass. It completely chokes out the native grasses and ground covers. And as far as I can tell, beyond providing shelter, the grass is not useful to wildlife. The seeds are not attractive to birds — when the snow is blowing and the natural seed crop is depleted or covered, even the tree sparrows and juncos ignore this plant. The white-tailed deer, which eat *everything* green, won't nibble on the sharp-edged leaves. In short, it is a noxious invader. We poison and burn and pull and mow it every chance we get. And each year, a few new patches spring up in our woods or meadow.

PURPLE CONEFLOWERS *provide nectar for butterflies in summer and seeds for finches and sparrows in winter.*

The pampas grass and other superinvaders (kudzu, Japanese bamboo, purple loosestrife, crown vetch, etc.) offer nothing to native birds and wildlife, yet they outcompete native plants that do offer food and shelter. As bird gardeners, we owe it to our birds and wildlife to plant native species and to battle non-native invasive species wherever we find them.

LEVELS AND TEXTURES

In selecting the plants to add to your bird-friendly landscape plan, go for a variety of layers. Choose plants of differing growth patterns and sizes and footprints (the amount of space they will take up when fully grown). Also consider the texture of your garden plan. You won't want tall trees blocking your view of shorter fruiting shrubs when the birds are eating the fruits. And you may not want the climbing native vines overtaking your flower garden just when the salvia is blooming and attracting hummingbirds. Variety is good, and it's even better with some planning. This is where a good resource on planning a bird-friendly garden—whether a landscaping expert or a reference book—will be helpful.

SEASONAL CHANGES

You'll also need to consider the seasonality of the plants you choose. Having everything thrive during the spring and summer is wonderful, but you'll be disappointed if your plant selection has little or nothing to offer birds in fall and winter. On our farm, we grow lots of native purple coneflowers in the flower gardens, and we encourage the native "weeds" in our meadow. Some of the best meadow plants are the goldenrods, ironweed, and bluestems. After blooming all summer long and giving us color in the form of flowers and the butterflies feeding on the flowers, these plants die with the frost. But they all continue to attract birds because each offers seeds for sparrows, towhees, and juncos. Walking through our meadow in late July, we'll scare up clouds of American goldfinches as they gather thistle down and milkweed "cotton" for their nests. In November, the same

WHEN WINTER strips the leaves off deciduous trees, our feeder birds use evergreens and our brush pile as shelter.

GIMME SHELTER

path will have dozens of tree, field, and white-throated sparrows, plus dark-eyed juncos and perhaps a surprise sparrow or two. In summer, the field sparrows and indigo buntings nest in the thicker meadow vegetation. These native plants, with a few non-invasive exotics, make our meadow a bird-friendly zone all year long.

Deciduous trees that lose their leaves in fall can seem barren in winter. We balance this in our yard with clumps of native pines. I started these clumps 17 years ago, digging up saplings under the mature stand of pines along our farm lane and transplanting them around the edges of our yard. We also have coniferous shrubs around our house foundation both as a windbreak from the weather and as shelter for our birds.

In winter we still have plenty of green vegetation in the form of pines and spruces and other conifers. Plus, we leave our weedy edges all around the yard, and that's where most of the winter bird action is centered. Our final yard mowing of the year is usually timed so that the grass has a chance to head out (or go to seed) before the first frost. Ground-feeding birds relish these grassy seed heads all winter long. When the snow covers the grass, the birds move to the weedy edges. When the weedy edges are snowed or iced under, the birds come to our various feeding stations.

Bird-friendly Plants

LETTING IT GO WILD

As I noted earlier, I am a big advocate of letting some part of a bird-friendly yard go wild. All this takes is the willpower to avoid mowing, trimming, or weeding a section of your property to see what comes up. You might be surprised. There are seeds in the soil of your yard that may have been lying dormant for years. There are plants that, given a chance to grow (with the cessation of regular mowing), may add immeasurably to the bird-attracting possibilities of your yard. But this does require a small bit of work on your part.

Here's a chance to use your bird-identifying skills on another set of living things: plants. You should know or be prepared to learn the identity of the plants in your yard and garden. Some of them may be amazing bird-friendly additions. Others will possibly be dastardly villains you will want to eliminate. There are excellent ID guides for plants, just as there are for birds. If this seems like a daunting project, enlist the help of a local master gardener or native-plant expert. These are people who, just like us bird watchers, know their subject

FOOD SOURCES, such as pokeweed fruit and the winged seeds of maple trees, occur naturally in many yards.

LETTING A PATCH of your yard grow out into its natural weedy state is good for birds and will reduce the area of lawn you need to maintain.

matter cold. My friend Jim is an excellent birder and also a world-class botanist. Every time Jim visits and we go for a walk around the farm, he points out plants I never knew we had—some native "keepers" and some exotics that I place on my Most Unwanted list. Jim's advice and plant identifications have been a big help over the years.

There are two basic ways you can go wild with a patch of your property. One is to simply let a section grow up fully through an entire growing season or even over several years, culling the unwanted plants and letting the good ones thrive. The second way is to select a patch of ground and cultivate it. That is, dig up the soil and turn it over, using a spade, fork, or hoe to break up the clumps of soil. Then watch to see what sprouts. You can sow some native, bird-friendly seeds or starter plants. Or you can see what the birds bring you by creating some "poop" perches. I've seen this done by erecting a series of snags for birds to use as perches, or by offering a fence rail or heavy-duty rope or cable thick and taut enough for perching birds to feel stable. This will concentrate the seed-carrying droppings of perching birds in your recently turned soil, and you'll get a bird-friendly garden patch courtesy of the birds. Be careful to weed out any undesirable plants as soon as they are grown out enough to identify—the birds may bring you a few things you don't want.

In our yard, we've gotten several interesting plants this way. A lovely tupelo tree, a fruit-bearing persimmon tree, countless sunflower plants, and several starts to grape vines were all "deposited" by our yard birds or dispersed by fruit and seed-eating mammals such as chipmunks and raccoons.

Bird-friendly plants

COMMON NAME	SCIENTIFIC NAME	GOOD FOR/OTHER NOTES
TREES		
Apples	*Malus* spp.	Fruit, insects, cavities
Ashes	*Fraxinus* spp.	Seeds, insects, cover
Aspens	*Populus* spp.	Seeds, insects, cover, cavities
Birches	*Betula* spp.	Seeds, insects, cover
Cedars	*Juniperus* spp.	Fruit, year-round cover
Cherries	*Prunus* spp.	Fruit
Chokecherry, common	*Prunus virginiana*	Fruit
Cottonwoods	*Populus* spp.	Cavities, shelter
Crab apples	*Malus* spp.	Fruit, insects
Dogwoods	*Cornus* spp.	Fruit
Firs	*Abies* spp.	Year-round cover
Hackberries	*Celtis* spp.	Fruit, cover
Hawthorns	*Crataegus* spp.	Fruit, cover, nesting
Hemlocks	*Tsuga* spp.	Seeds, insects, shelter
Hollies	*Ilex* spp.	Fruit, year-round cover
Junipers	*Juniperus* spp.	Year-round cover
Larches	*Larix* spp.	Seeds
Madrones	*Arbutus* spp.	Fruit
Maples	*Acer* spp.	Seeds, cover
Mesquites	*Prosopis* spp.	Shelter
Mountain ashes	*Sorbus* spp.	Fruit
Mulberry, red	*Morus rubra*	Fruit
Oaks	*Quercus* spp.	Acorns, cover
Pines	*Pinus* spp.	Year-round cover
Poplars	*Populus* spp.	Cavities, shelter
Sassafras	*Sassafras albidum*	Fruit, cover, cavities
Shadbush, or serviceberry	*Amelanchier laevis*	Fruit, flowers
Spruces	*Picea* spp.	Year-round cover
Sycamores	*Platanus* spp.	Cavities, shelter
Willows	*Salix* spp.	Cavities, shelter

COMMON NAME	SCIENTIFIC NAME	GOOD FOR/OTHER NOTES
SHRUBS		
Arrowwood viburnum	*Viburnum dentatum/Viburnum* spp.	Fall fruit. Shade tolerant
Bayberry, northern	*Myrica pensylvanica*	Fruit. Male, female needed for fruit
Blackberry, American	*Rubus allegheniensis*	Fruit, dense cover, nesting
Blueberry, highbush	*Vaccinium corymbosum*	Fruit, flower, cover. Acid soil
Chokeberry, red	*Aronia arbutifolia*	Fruit. Moist soil preferred
Cranberry, highbush	*Viburnum trilobum*	Fruit. Shade tolerant
Dogwood	*Cornus* spp.	Fall fruit, dense cover
Elderberry, American	*Sambucus canadensis*	Fruit, dense cover
Hercules' club	*Aralia spinosa*	Fruit attracts warblers, thrushes
Hobblebush	*Viburnum alnifolium*	Fruit. Shade tolerant
Holly, deciduous	*Ilex deciduas, Ilex* spp.	Winter fruit. Male, female needed for fruit
Huckleberry, black	*Gaylussacia baccata*	Fruit. Sandy soil preferred
Inkberry	*Ilex glabra*	Fruit. Thicket-forming. Acid soil
Mahonia	*Mahonia aquifolium*	Fruit, year-round cover
Manzanitas	*Arcostaphylos* spp.	Early fruit, thick cover
Nannyberry	*Viburnum lentago*	Fruit. Shade tolerant
Pokeweed	*Phytolacca americana*	Fall fruit
Roses	*Rosa* spp.	Winter fruits, summer flowers
Shadbush	*Amelanchier* spp.	Early fruit
Spicebush	*Lindera benzoin*	Fruit. Moist soil
Sumac	*Rhus* spp.	Fruit available all winter
Winterberry, common	*Ilex verticillata*	Fruit. Male, female needed for fruit
Yew	*Taxus* spp.	Year-round cover, some fruit

COMMON NAME	SCIENTIFIC NAME	GOOD FOR/OTHER NOTES
VINES		
Grape, wild	*Vitis* spp.	Fruit attracts 100 species, cover
Greenbrier	*Smilax* spp.	Fruit, thick cover
Honeysuckle	*Lonicera* spp. (native only)	Nectar, fruit, cover. **Avoid Asian spp.**
Trumpet vine	*Campsis radicans*	Nectar, summer cover
Virginia creeper	*Parthenocissus quinquefolia*	Fruit attracts 40 species

COMMON NAME	SCIENTIFIC NAME	GOOD FOR/OTHER NOTES
FLOWERS		
Asters	*Symphyotrichum* spp.	Flowers attract butterflies, seed
Bachelor's button	*Centaurea cyanus*	Seed
Black-eyed Susan	*Rudbeckia serotina*	Seed
Blazing star	*Liatris* spp.	Seed, flowers attract butterflies
California poppy	*Eschscholzia californica*	Seed
Coneflower, purple	*Echinacea purpurea*	Seed, flowers attract butterflies
Coreopsis	*Coreopsis* spp.	Seed, flowers attract butterflies
Cosmos	*Cosmos* spp.	Seed
Goldenrods	*Solidago* spp.	Flowers for butterflies, winter cover
Joe-pye weed	*Eupatorium* spp.	Flowers for butterflies, winter cover
Marigolds	*Tagetes* spp.	Seed
Penstemons	*Penstemon* spp.	Nectar, seed
Poppies	*Papaver* spp.	Flowers attract butterflies, seed
Primrose	*Oenothera* spp.	Seed
Sedums	*Sedum* spp.	Flowers attract butterflies, seed
Sunflowers	*Helianthus* spp.	Seed, esp. downy, Maximilian, western sunflower
Thistle, globe	*Echinops* spp.	Flowers, seed, nesting material
Zinnias	*Zinnia elegans*	Seed, flowers attract butterflies

WHAT WILL THE NEIGHBORS SAY?

We live at the end of a long lane, well off the gravel township road, so I don't ever get complaints from my neighbors about what we're doing (or not doing) with our yard. But your situation might be different if you live in a nice suburb with neighbors close by. Sad to say, much of the expansion of human housing has been into rural and wild areas that were formerly the home of many species of birds and wildlife. Sometimes we forget this. I get a dozen calls each year from homeowners who are anxious to know how they can keep the woodpeckers from drilling holes in their wooden siding. I tell them "Well, to a woodpecker, your house looks like a giant tree! And come fall, the woodpecker may try to excavate a roosting cavity in your siding!" We need to coexist with our avian neighbors as well as with our human neighbors.

The typical subdivision in North America usually starts with a bulldozer clearing off all the trees and brush. Then, nice rectangular lots are laid out and flagged and the building begins. Houses are erected, and they look like alien spaceships plopped down in a sea of new turf—lonely and out of place. Then the developer or homeowner decides to "landscape" by placing a few saplings in the front and back yard, staked in place with support ropes, with round holes cut in the turf around their trunks.

IN WOODLAND AREAS, any natural cavity in a large tree may become a nesting or roosting site for screech-owls. These are western screech-owl nestlings.

Nice! It's a dream come true for some lucky family.

But the opposite is true if you are one of the 40 or so species of birds that lived there before the bulldozer. This landscape now has almost nothing to offer you. Even if a bird feeder is placed on a hook atop a metal pole in the middle of the yard, it's not going to make the place that much more attractive to the birds.

Those of us who avoid this kind of sterile suburban moonscape know that not everyone thinks as we do. Not everyone *wants* birds and wildlife. These always seem to be the folks who live right next door, too. It's our special cross to bear to help these folks understand what we are doing in our yards and gardens to attract wildlife. And all it takes is a few conversations. Explain why you leave your dead garden plants standing all winter—the birds love the seeds and insects the garden provides. The brushy, brambly corner of your yard or the hedgerow you've let grow are there to give the birds a place to rest, to roost, and to nest. You're sure to impress your neighbors when you explain that the dead tree you are letting remain in your yard is home to a family of chickadees or screech-owls. Show them your ever-expanding bird list as proof that your efforts are bearing fruit—literally and figuratively.

You will encounter some neatniks who will never be convinced. But most neighbors, if they are *good* neighbors, will support what you're trying to do in making your yard more bird-friendly. Besides, it's a known fact that a backyard filled with bird song on a spring morning vastly increases property values.

RATIONALE FOR A MORE NATURAL YARD

If you follow the ideas in this book, you may find yourself feeling defensive about your natural-looking yard. Perhaps a neighbor has made a passing comment about loaning you his mower, or the head of your housing development's property maintenance board has said she's received complaints about your patches of long grass. I would never encourage you to ignore local ordinances or guidelines, of course. But I will give you a few useful and informative statements to help your neighbors understand why you're doing what you're doing.

1. YOU ARE SAVING THE PLANET. Less mowing and weed-whacking is good for the environment in several ways: It reduces consumption of fossil fuels and output of damaging exhaust that contributes to harmful greenhouse gases. Furthermore, the living plant material, or biomass, in your yard is turning carbon dioxide into breathable oxygen for the entire neighborhood.

2. NATURAL IS BETTER. By letting parts of your property "go natural," you are avoiding the need to use expensive and potentially harmful chemicals for lawn maintenance. The native plants you have landscaped with are perfectly adapted for your region's climate, thus reducing the amount of water needed to keep them alive. Nothing wastes more water than keeping a lawn green in a dry summer. Native plants are adapted to wet and dry climate cycles.

3. NATURE IS GOOD FOR YOU. Dozens of scientific studies have shown that people with easy access to the natural world—even a small patch of flowers or a single blooming fruit tree—are mentally and physically healthier than those who lack such access. Watching nature in all its subtle glory is relaxing and fascinating. Keeping a list of the creatures and plants you observe in your yard demonstrates the rich environment you've created and can help sharpen your mind at the same time.

These are just three of the many reasons you can give to justify your natural landscaping. You may think of others that work better for your situation. But be prepared to accept your role as the neighborhood nature expert once others realize how wonderful your yard really is.

DEALING WITH PROBLEM PLANTS

Many of the problems you'll encounter while transforming your yard will involve the conflict between which plants are good for birds and which are not. Again, this is where having good reference material or helpful advice from a knowledgeable source is key.

I am a vocal opponent of lawn and garden chemicals. We use organic sprays only on our houseplants and never outside. I do resort to the use of a fast-degrading herbicide (Roundup is one brand) to kill our pampas grass when I find it. I spot spray it on the plant I want to kill. I am careful to do this on a day with no wind while the plant is still growing. The grass takes the herbicide into its system, and within a few days it is brown. I try to do this before the plant can set seed. If I could pull the grass out I would, but that is impossible.

We also have a horrible problem with Japanese wisteria, which grew around the foundation of the old farmhouse that once stood a few hundred feet from our current house. Every summer I engage in a fit of cutting, pulling, and disentangling—trying to hold the nasty vine at bay. This plant is very invasive, and I'm already contemplating my strategy for next summer. So far, the wisteria is winning.

If you are a member of a local bird or garden club, its members can be an excellent resource not only for problem solving but for advice on what plants work best for birds in your region.

OVER TIME YOU'LL LEARN

Perhaps the best teachers are time and experience. Over time, you'll learn what works best in your own yard, as well as which plants you and your birds like most. Remember that just because a plant does not produce fruit or seeds for a bird to eat does not mean it isn't bird-friendly. Many plants attract insects that birds eat. Plants with thick vegetative growth patterns are good sources of shelter from weather and predators and are safe places to build a nest and raise a family.

Keeping notes about which species you've planted and where can be useful. We frequently refer to a rough drawing we made of our property and how we planned to add plants and elements to the yard. Try this yourself. It does not have to be done in extreme detail. In late winter, when the gardening catalogs arrive, you can turn to your yard design and notes to begin planning for the bird-friendly gardening season ahead.

AMONG THE INVASIVE PLANTS *we battle on our farm is Japanese wisteria, an exotic species from Asia.*

Chapter 5 Bird Housing

WHEN MOST PEOPLE THINK OF A BIRD HOUSE, they imagine one of those brown wooden structures, perhaps decorated with gingerbread trim, and with a tiny entrance hole, hanging on a low branch of the apple tree out back. There are a few problems with this bucolic image. First of all, it's very likely that the house was designed with human style preferences in mind rather than the needs and preferences of the birds. Second, in many parts of the continent, placing a bird house on or in a tree is more an act of offering an easy meal to predators than helping cavity-nesting birds.

In this chapter, we'll take a short tour through the world of natural bird homes and human-supplied housing with a few side trips into ways you can be a better landlord to the birds in your backyard.

Natural Homes

In North America north of the United States–Mexico border, about 85 species of birds are considered to be primarily cavity nesters. Cavity nesters are birds that nest inside enclosed spaces, such as inside a hollow tree branch, trunk, or log; inside an excavated hole (such as one drilled by a woodpecker); or even inside a human-supplied nest box. This makes cavity nesters different than most of our wild birds, which build some sort of open-cup nest or perhaps nest on the ground.

Because they are enclosed on all sides, nest cavities provide greater protection from the elements and from predators than do open-cup or ground nests. With this greater protection, cavity-nesting birds are afforded a longer period of development. The nestlings of cavity-nesting birds need between 16 and 22 days from hatching (leaving the egg) to fledging (leaving the nest). Open-nesting species take just 9 to 14 days from hatching to fledgling. Without the added protection that a cavity nest affords, open-nesting birds must get feathered and out much more quickly in order to survive.

The vast majority of cavity nesters use naturally occurring cavities for their nest sites. Woodpeckers are the leading source of nesting cavities. They use their chisel-like bills to excavate a new nesting cavity for themselves each spring. They may also excavate roosting cavities in addition to their nest holes. While their roost holes may be used year after year, most woodpecker nest holes are not reused by the same pair or family of birds. This frees up these "used" nest cavities for other creatures. Although chickadees, nuthatches, and titmice can excavate nesting cavities in very soft or rotting wood, they most often rely on natural cavities or old woodpecker holes.

If you've followed the bird-friendly suggestions in the previous four chapters, you are already offering plenty of nesting habitat for open-cup nesters. One of the best ways to encourage cavity-nesting birds is to have a stand of large trees. If you already have large trees on your property, it's likely that some parts of those trees—or perhaps one or more of the trees themselves—are dead or dying. If you can—and I know it can be hard—resist the urge to cut down dead trees and to trim out large dead branches. Dead and dying wood is often ideal for cavity excavation by woodpeckers. Of course, if a large dead tree is looming over your house, ready to destroy your roof by crashing down in the next storm, you need to remove it.

I had a friend in Maryland with this very conundrum: a perfectly good (and dead) oak tree near his house. This tree

A MALE GOLDEN-FRONTED WOODPECKER in a nest hole.

had several hollows and woodpecker holes that were regularly used by woodpeckers, screech-owls, great crested flycatchers, flying squirrels, and once by a pair of wood ducks. But the tree got weaker near its base and became a prime candidate for removal. The tree did come down, but not before a hole was dug farther away from the house. The trunk and several key branches stayed intact, and the whole unit was dropped into the new anchor hole with the help of the tree removal company. Cement held the giant snag in place, and the next spring Carolina chickadees nested in one of the old woodpecker holes.

Not everyone wants to go to this much effort to save a dead tree. And many people do not have trees large enough to support a nest cavity. This next section is for them.

Bird Houses

If you look out your window and see a large treeless expanse of grass, there is one quick thing you can do to enhance its bird appeal: put up nest boxes. Our three species of bluebirds and tree and violet-green swallows are among the cavity nesters that readily take to human-supplied housing in the form of nest boxes (or if you prefer, bird houses).

Before you begin sticking bird houses up willy-nilly, you need to take the four Ps under consideration.

1. PROPER HOUSING: All cavity-nesting birds have specific needs.

2. PROPER PLACEMENT: Place the housing in the right habitat and in the right setting.

3. PESTICIDES: Never use lawn and garden chemicals in a yard with nest boxes—they are potentially lethal to adult and nestling birds.

4. PREDATORS: Mounting boxes with predator deterrence in mind is essential in many parts of the continent.

NEST-BOX BASICS

Whether you buy your nest boxes at a store or build them from scratch, there are certain characteristics your housing should have to best suit the birds' needs. Here are some recommendations for nest-box basics.

• The lumber should be untreated and at least ¾ inch thick to protect nests from spring chills and summer heat. Exterior plywood, red cedar, and pine work well. Other, less durable woods can work well, too, if the external surfaces are treated with weatherproof paint or stain.

• Do not paint or stain the inside of the box. If you paint or stain the outside, use a light earth tone so sunlight and heat will be reflected, not absorbed.

• Use galvanized screws to assemble the nest box. It will last years longer than one built with nails or glue, which will rapidly lose their hold as the wood warps and shrinks.

- You should have easy access to the inside of the nest box for inspections and maintenance. The best box designs feature a side or front panel that swings up or out for access to the inside.

- Perches on the front of a nest box are not necessary. All cavity nesters have strong feet and can easily cling to vertical wooden surfaces. Perches only give easy access to house sparrows, starlings, and predators.

- The roof of the nest box should extend well over the entrance hole to protect it from driving rain and from the reach of predators.

- The inside front panel of the box should be deeply scored below the hole to give emerging nestlings an easier toehold for exiting the box.

A FEMALE EASTERN BLUEBIRD arrives at a nest box with food for her nestlings.

- The floor of the nest box should have at least four ³⁄₈-inch drain holes so the box can drain if it does get wet. The floor should be recessed so that no end grain is exposed to soak up water in wet weather.

- Ventilation holes near the top allow excess heat to escape. Plug these same holes with weather-stripping putty in cold weather.

- The nest box should be protected from predators. The best way to protect your nest boxes is to mount them on poles with a predator baffle below the box.

- Refer to the accompanying table of cavity-nesting birds for information about each species' preferences for housing size, entry-hole diameter, and placement.

UNIVERSAL BIRD HOUSING

An all-purpose nest box that works well for a variety of species is one that has an interior dimension of 8 inches in depth with sides between 4 and 6 inches in width. The entrance hole is 1½ inches in diameter.

Reference chart for cavity-nesting birds

SPECIES	INTERIOR FLOOR SIZE OF BOX (INCHES)	INTERIOR HEIGHT OF BOX (INCHES)	ENTRANCE-HOLE DIAMETER (INCHES)	MOUNT BOX THIS HIGH (FEET)
Chickadees	4x4	9–12	1⅛–1½	5–15
Titmice	4x4	12	1½	5–12
White-breasted nuthatch	4x4	12	1½	5–12
Carolina wren	4x4	9–12	1–1½	5–10
Eastern bluebird	4x4	12	1½	5–6
Western bluebird	5x5	12	1½–1⁹⁄₁₆	5–6
Mountain bluebird	5x5	12	1⁹⁄₁₆	5–6
Tree swallow	5x5	10–12	1½	5–10
Violet-green swallow	5x5	10–12	1½	5–10
Purple martin	6x6	6	2⅛	15–25
House finch	5x5	10	1½	5–10
Downy woodpecker	4x4	12	1½	5–20
Hairy woodpecker	6x6	14	1½	8–20
Red-bellied woodpecker	6x6	14	2	8–20
Golden-fronted woodpecker	6x6	14	2	8–20
Red-headed woodpecker	6x6	14	2	8–20
Northern flicker	7x7	16–24	2½	10–20
Pileated woodpecker	12x12	24	4	15–25
Wood duck, mergansers, goldeneyes	12x12	24	3x4	5*–20
Screech-owls	8x8	18	3	8–30

*over water; mount higher over land

HOUSE WREN nesting in a wren house.

ALL NEST BOXES — Sizes above are minimum ideal sizes for each species. Interior height refers to inside back panel. Always baffle nest boxes.

WREN BOXES — Larger, oblong holes make it easier to get twigs into box.

SWALLOW BOXES — Carve grooves or place hardware cloth on inside of front of box.

PURPLE MARTIN BOXES — Size listed here is for one compartment in a multiunit martin house. See *Enjoying Purple Martins More*, published by BWD Press.

DUCK BOXES — Add 3" of wood chips to floor of box. Staple 5"-wide hardware cloth "ladder" directly under hole on inside of box. Mount boxes higher when not placed over water.

WOODPECKER BOXES — Pack cavity full with wood chips and sawdust.

OWL BOXES — Add 3" of wood chips to floor of box.

HABITAT FOR BOX PLACEMENT	COMMENTS
Open woods, edges	A 1⅛" hole excludes all other birds except house sparrows.
Wooded areas, edges	A 1⅛" hole excludes all other birds except house sparrows.
Wooded areas, edges	Other nuthatch species may prefer a 1¼" hole.
Old-fields, thickets	House wren 1" hole, Bewick's wren 1¼" hole.
Open land with scattered trees	See *Enjoying Bluebirds More*, published by BWD Press.
Open land with scattered trees	
Open meadows above 5,000 ft.	
Open land near pond or lake	Place "escape ladder" on inside front of box. See below.
Pastures, fields, parks	
Open country near water	Entrance hole 1" above floor. See comments below.
Backyards, porches	Often nests in hanging plants.
Forest openings, edges	
Forest openings, edges	
Forest openings, edges	
Forest openings, edges	
Forest openings, edges	
Farmland, open country	
Mature forest	
Wooded swamps, bottomland	Hole is a horizontally oriented oval.
Farmland, orchards, woods	

HOUSE PLACEMENT

Once you have acquired housing, you'll need to place it in the right habitat. Having selected a spot in appropriate habitat, make certain your nest boxes are securely mounted and baffled against predators (more about this topic on page 68). Some species, such as martins and swallows, also require a clear flight path to and from the nest-box entrance.

If you are placing your nest box on a baffled pole, face the box away from the prevailing wind. This will ensure that precipitation and wind do not blow directly into the entrance hole. If you look carefully for nest holes drilled by woodpeckers, you'll see that they are most often found on the lee side (away from prevailing wind and weather) of a tree,

NEST BOXES *placed in open habitat are less attractive to aggressive cavity-nest competitors such as house wrens, European starlings, and house sparrows.*

often below a sheltering branch. Mounting the nest box at least 5 feet off the ground will keep the nest out of leaping range for cats, squirrels, and raccoons, but you'll still be able to see inside the box during your nest checks.

Bluebirds and tree and violet-green swallows prefer houses placed in open grassy areas, mounted 5 feet or more above the ground. Screech-owls and wood ducks prefer large nest boxes placed high in large trees, though they may accept housing or natural cavities in other settings. House wrens, chickadees, and titmice prefer houses placed in the woods or along a wooded edge.

Being a Good Landlord

Now that you are about to become a landlord to your backyard birds, you have a few ongoing responsibilities. You will need to maintain your housing through the seasons. Birds often use nest boxes well beyond the nesting season for nighttime roosting and for shelter during inclement weather. You'll need to keep records of what's happening and not happening in your nest boxes. You'll have to clean out the nest boxes when they become soiled with bird droppings and the other detritus of the breeding season. And you'll have to protect your birds from harm as much as possible. Harm will certainly come to some of them, at which point you will need to become a crime-scene detective to try to determine what happened and how to prevent it from happening again.

LOOKING INTO A NEST BOX

You slowly open a nest box and see a black-capped chickadee sitting on its nest. What do you do? Simply close the box, walk away, and record in your notebook that the female was on the nest, probably incubating eggs. This scenario underscores the reason nest boxes should be easy to open from the front or side. If you spend several minutes disassembling a nest box to check its contents, that can be enough to drive a nesting bird away permanently. If a bird leaves as you approach or as you open the box, inspect the nest quickly, record your findings, and leave the area. Your complete visit should take no more than a few minutes. If you are able to keep your visit this brief, the bird will return to the nest box shortly. You may even want to watch from about 30 yards away and time how long it takes for the parent to return to the nest.

After the eggs hatch and the parents are bringing food to the chicks every few minutes, you may also want to record their comings and goings. If you know which species is using your nest box, you can find information about its incubation period. If you know the approximate date that egg laying ended and incubation began, you can estimate the hatching date of the eggs. This is important information. Timing is everything for a nest-box landlord. If you visit the nest during incubation or late in the nestling stage, you may cause nest abandonment or premature fledging. A good general rule is to limit nest-box visits to the 12 days immediately after hatching. Resist the urge to visit nestlings—appealing as they may be—more often than necessary.

MONITORING YOUR NEST BOXES

Observing and recording the progress of active nests is perhaps the most fascinating aspect of being a landlord to cavity-nesting birds. For most of the nesting season, a weekly visit to each box will provide an accurate snapshot of the lives of your birds, without undue disturbance.

BLUEBIRD EGGS are pale sky-blue.

If you have more than a couple of nest boxes on your property, or if you've placed nest boxes in a series, as many bluebird enthusiasts do, it's a good idea to number the boxes to keep accurate records. Bluebird trail operators, some of whom have hundreds of nest boxes along roadways, on golf courses, and in parks, have perfected the science of monitoring nest boxes and keeping accurate records. They can tell you, for example, how many eggs are in each box, and how many fledglings box #32 has fledged over the past five years. Like bird watching itself, the hobby of being a conscientious landlord to cavity-nesting birds can become addictive.

CHICKADEE NESTS almost always contain moss and animal hair among the construction materials. These Carolina chickadees are just a few days from fledging.

RECORDING YOUR OBSERVATIONS

Here's how to record your observations: Devote a separate field notebook to your nest boxes, allowing several pages per nest box. Record what you see during your nest-box inspections. Include the following information: Is the box being used? By what species? Has courtship or nest building begun? If there is a nest in the box, what is it made of? If there are eggs, how many and what do they look like?

BAFFLING PREDATORS

IN AREAS where snakes and climbing mammals are predators of bird nests, it is important to mount nest boxes on poles with predator baffles.

Putting up a nest box and hoping for the best is not really being a good landlord to the birds. In fact, if it seems like too much work to have to check and maintain your nest box or boxes, I suggest you not take it on. Stick to bird feeding. Being a good landlord requires some effort and commitment.

Nesting birds face long odds: the vast majority of nesting attempts by wild birds end in failure. Weather, predation, disease, competition, parasitism—all of these can cause a nesting attempt to fail. It is neither practical nor possible for us to ensure the success of all the birds nesting in our backyards, but we can at least help out the ones using the bird houses and nesting sites we provide.

The leading cause of nesting failure among cavity-nesting birds is predation. Birds, their eggs, and their young are a sought-after meal for many predators. Mammals of all sizes, from field mice to bears, will predate birds' nests, as will snakes and even other birds. This may seem like unfair odds until you realize that it's fairly easy to keep predators away from the tasty birds inside your nest boxes.

A nest box nailed to a fencepost or a tree trunk is perfectly safe in a few parts of North America where climbing predators are scarce. Mountain bluebird boxes nailed to fenceposts in the high desert of the West seem to produce excellent breeding success. But for most of the continent, a nest box nailed to a tree or fencepost is nothing more than a feeding station for wily predators. I have seen bluebird trails with dozens of houses mounted along highway fences. Every single house had its roof or door ripped off by a hungry raccoon.

Here on our farm in southeastern Ohio, a nest in a box on a fencepost will get cleaned out by a raccoon or a black snake before the eggs even hatch. So we mount all of our nest boxes on poles, with predator baffles on the poles below the house.

Pole-mounted housing has several advantages. First of all, we can place the nest boxes exactly where we want them. Second, we can move them if necessary. Third, a pole-mounted predator baffle is very effective in this type of set-up.

Pole-mounted predator baffles prevent a predator such as a house cat, raccoon, chipmunk, or snake from getting up the pole to the nest box. When designed and mounted properly, they are as close to 100 percent effective as a baffle can get.

But not every predator needs to climb the pole to access the nest. Common grackles, blue jays, American crows, and even some owls can fly right up to the box and reach inside. This is where proper box construction can help. Nest boxes constructed with wood at least 1 inch thick and with a floor that is at least 6 inches (and preferably more) below the entrance hole make it difficult for a bird to reach inside to get at eggs or young. An overhanging roof will foil most avian predators. Some well-made boxes even feature wood or other materials that extend the entrance hole outward, making it more difficult for any predator to reach a claw or bill inside the box. These entry extensions do not seem to bother the nesting birds at all, but they also do nothing to stop raccoons or snakes.

WHEN THINGS GO WRONG

Sooner or later you will open your nest box and find dead nestlings or even dead adult birds, or see that eggs are missing. These things can happen because of harsh weather, disease, or territorial competition with other cavity-nesting birds. House sparrows and house wrens are two of the most territorial cavity nesters. They will often destroy the nests of rival cavity nesters. House sparrows will even kill competing birds by pecking their heads with their strong bills. For this reason, many bluebird landlords do not tolerate the non-native house sparrows anywhere near their boxes.

CONSCIENTIOUS LANDLORDS check their nest boxes regularly to remove parasites, exchange nesting material, and monitor the health of nestlings.

European starlings are fierce competitors for nesting cavities, but they are too large to fit inside a box with an entrance hole 1½ inches in diameter or smaller. This aggressive non-native species often takes over larger boxes, such as those intended for flycatchers, purple martins, northern flickers, or American kestrels.

Decades of field experimentation by veteran nest-box landlords have resulted in a variety of strategies to thwart unwanted competition by non-native species. If you are facing an ugly competition for your nest boxes, tap into the information available online and in print from one of the state, regional, provincial, or national cavity-nesting bird organizations. The North American Bluebird Society and the Purple Martin Conservation Association are two such organizations. Contact information for both is in the Resources section at the back of this book.

CLEANING OUT AND WINTERIZING NEST BOXES

There has been quite a bit of debate over the years about whether or not to clean out nest boxes at the end of the nesting season. I've always been an advocate of doing so. Some landlords believe that a house with a remnant nest in it is more attractive to prospecting birds in spring.

WHEN A BROOD HAS FLEDGED, *it is a good idea to clean out the old nest. Some landlords like to place a handful of clean, dry grass in the cleaned-out box. This provides roosting birds with a bit of insulation during cold weather.*

They may think it gives these potential tenants a visual clue that this is a successful nest site. I hedge my bets by replacing the old dirty nest with a similar-sized cup of clean, dried grass. This gives the birds some insulation during winter and nighttime roosting. And it may serve as a starter foundation for next year's nest, though most cavity-nesting species seem to remove old nesting material before constructing their own nests.

Before putting in the cup of dry grass, we scrape out and wash the box interior if necessary. If it's looking like the wood is getting overly weathered, I repaint the outside of the box with a solid body stain. I then caulk the box's ventilation holes with strips of claylike window putty, to keep the winter wind from howling in. It gives me a sense of satisfaction to know that our birds will have a cozy shelter all winter long. Discarded seeds and bird droppings, plus the occasional shed feather, are clues that tell us that birds use our nest boxes all winter long.

Nesting Myths

Human history is clotted with examples of misinformation. And today we have our friend the Internet to help us spread these myths. In this section, I'll deal with some of the most common ones about bird housing.

> **Myth:** *Checking a nest box will cause the parents to abandon the nest.*
> **Reality:** Regular, brief nest-box checks will not disturb the nesting birds. Check during the day when the weather is good. That way, even if the parent incubating the eggs or brooding the nestlings leaves when you open the box, there will be little danger of damage. Once the nestlings are 12 days post-hatching, stop visiting until

after fledging occurs. If you don't know the age of eggs or young, observe the nest from a distance to examine the birds safely.

Myth: *Handling eggs or young birds in a nest will leave your human smell on them, and the adults will abandon them.*

Reality: Scientists continue to argue about the olfactory ability of birds. Some birds, such as vultures, appear to have a well-developed sense of smell. Most songbirds probably do not have a pronounced sense of smell. But predators of birds' nests certainly do. Mammals and snakes can follow the scent to an unprotected nest box for an easy meal. This is why it's important to baffle your nest boxes if you live in an area where these predators exist.

IT IS FINE TO HANDLE NESTLINGS for a short time while checking or changing a nest, but your hands should be clean and free of chemicals.

Myth: *I don't need a baffle on my nest boxes.*

Reality: It's true that there are parts of North America where nest-box predators are rare and boxes placed on fenceposts and tree trunks can go unmolested for years. For most of the continent, however, it's better to be safe than sorry. The first time you open a box expecting to see cute baby birds and instead find them missing, or at least parts of them missing, you'll wish you had baffled.

Myth: *I've had the same pair of (chickadees, bluebirds, woodpeckers, owls, wood ducks) nesting in my nest box for 10 years.*

Reality: It's not impossible for this to be the case, but it's highly unlikely. Most backyard birds are relatively short-lived. The bluebirds that nest in your box each spring are more likely to be either the offspring or opportunistic neighbors of your original pair.

Myth: *Sure, I have house sparrows nesting near my bluebird boxes, but I've never had any trouble with them.*

Reality: When the house sparrow population runs out of nesting spots, it will begin to get more aggressive about stealing nest sites from your more deserving birds, such as chickadees, titmice, bluebirds, swallows, and wrens.

Myth: *I take down my nest boxes in fall because the birds use them only during the nesting season.*

Reality: Birds use many nest boxes for nighttime roosting during the fall and winter. It's both wise and helpful to keep your houses up year-round. This also ensures that the boxes will be available in spring as soon as your nesting birds begin their courtship.

Ten Things You Can Do to Help Nesting Birds

Spring is the start of the breeding season for most North American birds. They pair up with mates, build nests, lay eggs, raise young, and then some of them repeat the cycle—as many as three times. There are some things you can do to assist your backyard birds at this busy time of year. Here they are, in the time-honored Top Ten format.

1. Keep your cat inside (and ask your neighbors to do the same). Cats take an incredible toll on songbirds, and species that nest in low places and their young are especially vulnerable to cat predation. Do the birds a favor and keep this unnatural predator away from places where birds nest.

2. Provide nest boxes. It may seem obvious, but a well-placed nest box can mean the difference between nesting success and failure for a cavity-nesting bird. It's hard for many species to compete with starlings and house sparrows, which can take all the best cavities.

3. Hold off trimming hedges and shrubs. Lots of species use small hedges and shrubs for nesting. If you see a bird building a nest in such a place on your property, you've got a great excuse to avoid this bit of yard work for the next month or two.

4. Put out short pieces of string and yarn. For birds that build woven nests (orioles, some sparrows, robins, and others), a few short pieces of yarn can come in mighty handy during building time. Offer the pieces in an onion bag or a small basket. Keep the pieces shorter than 2 inches to reduce the risk of birds getting tangled in them.

5. Offer pet or human hair in onion bags or obvious places. If you looked at a hundred bird nests, chances are that most of them would have some animal hair in them. It's soft, insulating, and easy to gather. When you groom your pet (or when you yourself are groomed), save the hair to spread around your backyard for the birds to use.

6. Put out eggshells for birds. Eggshells help female birds replace calcium lost during egg production and laying. Save your eggshells, dry them out in the oven (30 minutes at 250 degrees), crumble them into small pieces, and spread them on an open spot on the ground.

7. Offer modest amounts of high-protein foods, such as mealworms, peanuts, suet dough, and suet, during periods of inclement weather. These foods may help nesting birds when weather makes other natural foods unavailable.

8. Don't mow meadows or brushy areas between late April and mid-August. We keep our farm fields long and grassy all summer long, mowing only a few paths that we keep short all year. This means that field sparrows, prairie warblers, meadowlarks, and other birds can nest in peace. And our box turtles, butterflies, rabbits, deer, foxes, and other creatures appreciate our "farming" style too.

9. If you find a nest, stay away. If you happen upon a bird's nest, don't linger, and don't make a return visit. We human beings leave scent trails wherever we go, and these scent trails can mean an easy meal for a hungry raccoon, opossum, fox, or other predator. (We leave the same trails to our outdoor pet-food dishes, garbage cans, and compost piles.) These predators are smart enough to follow these trails to see if they might lead to a snack. For the birds' sake, don't help blow a nest's cover by visiting it repeatedly.

TITMICE, like chickadees, line their nests with soft hair or fur. This tufted titmouse is yanking on a wad of goat hair.

10. Provide water for bathing and drinking on hot days. Provide water all year long if you can—but make sure to keep it clean. Your birdbath may be the first place in your backyard a parent bird takes its offspring. Lots of family-style bathing takes place at summer birdbaths, and young birds can be dependent on the only water source they know. So keep your bath filled and clean. Make sure the average water depth is less than 3 inches. Birds appreciate shallow water.

Chapter 6
Some Special Customers

WHETHER THEY CHOOSE TO ADMIT IT OR NOT, most backyard bird watchers have one or more species that are their favorites. I admit to a few of mine. I can't wait for the first ruby-throated hummingbird of spring. The spring feeder visits from rose-breasted grosbeaks and indigo buntings thrill me. The first dark-eyed junco of fall arrives in mid-October, and the first fox sparrow is found scratching under our spruce tree a few weeks later. I also get a charge when a yellow-bellied sapsucker visits the peanut feeder or the suet log. And I never get tired of feeding suet dough and mealworms to our eastern bluebirds in winter. Is that list long enough for you? Because I could go on . . .

In this chapter we'll explore some of the special birds that visit our feeders, along with how we can offer them things they need and want so we get to enjoy them more often.

Hummingbirds

Find me a person who does not like hummingbirds. I'll bet you can't. Even people who don't like birds like hummingbirds. Why? I think it's because hummingbirds are completely amazing, captivating creatures. They verge on the magical. Their flying ability is second to none in the avian world. How many birds can fly backward, upside down, in a corkscrew or looping pattern, and can hover—all in the space of a few seconds? Answer: One.

Sixteen hummingbird species regularly breed in North America north of the Mexico border. Of these, just seven or eight have significantly large breeding ranges, and just one, the ruby-throated hummingbird, breeds in the eastern half of the continent. Most of our hummingbirds, or hummers as we birders often call them, live and breed in the West.

Hummingbirds are our smallest birds. The largest, 5¼ inches in length from bill tip to tail end, is the magnificent hummingbird. The smallest is the Calliope hummingbird, at just 3¼ inches. Named for the whirring hum of their wings, hummingbirds use their flying and hovering ability to access nectar in flowering plants. Their needlelike bill probes tubular flowers for nectar, which their specially adapted tongue laps up. Brightly colored throat feathers, called gorgets, adorn most of the adult males. These gaudy colors, which reflect sunlight in flashes, are used to communicate during courtship with potential mates and in territorial disputes with rival males.

Plants to attract hummingbirds

KEY TO REGIONS
CN Canadian North **CE** Continental East **M/GP** Midwest/Great Plains **MW** Mountain West **DW** Desert West
PCN Pacific Coast—Northwest **PCC** Pacific Coast—California **HS** Humid South

COMMON NAME	SCIENTIFIC NAME	REGION
ANNUALS AND PERENNIALS		
Anise sage	*Salvia guaranitica*	CE, M/GP, MW, DW, PCC, HS
Autumn sage	*Salvia greggii*	CE, MW, DW, PCC, HS
Bee balm, or bergamot	*Monarda didyma* or *M. citriodora*	CN, CE, M/GP, MW, DW, PCN, PCC, HS
Bleeding heart	*Dicentra spectabilis* or *D. eximia*	CE, M/GP, MW, DW, PCN
Butterfly weed	*Asclepias tuberosa*	CN, CE, M/GP, MW, DW, PCC, HS
Canna lily	*Canna* spp. and hybrids	CN, CE, M/GP, MW, DW, PCN, PCC, HS
Cardinal flower	*Lobelia cardinalis*	CN, CE, M/GP, MW, DW, PCN, PCC, HS
Chuparosa	*Justicia californica*	DW, PCC
Columbine	*Aquilegia* spp.	CN, CE, M/GP, MW, DW, PCN, PCC, HS
Coralbells	*Heuchera sanguinea*	CN, CE, M/GP, MW, DW, PCN, PCC, HS
Daylily	*Hemerocallis* spp.	CN, CE, M/GP, MW, DW, PCN, PCC, HS
Delphinium, or scarlet larkspur	*Delphinium cardinale*	CN, CE, M/GP, MW, PCN, PCC, HS
Four o'clock	*Mirabilis jalapa*	CN, CE, M/GP, MW, DW, PCN, PCC, HS
Foxglove	*Digitalis* spp.	CN, CE, M/GP, MW, PCN, PCC, HS
Fuchsia	*Fuchsia lycoides*	CN, CE, M/GP, MW, PCN, PCC
Gladiolus	*Gladiolus* spp.	CN, CE, M/GP, MW, PCC, HS
Hollyhock	*Alcea rosea*	CN, CE, M/GP, MW, PCN, PCC, HS
Hosta, or plantain lily	*Hosta* spp.	CE, M/GP, MW, PCN, HS
Hummingbird trumpet	*Epilobium californica* or *E. cana*	MW, DW, PCN, PCC
Hyssop	*Agastache mexicana, A. berberi,* or *A. cana*	CE, M/GP, MW, DW, PCN, PCC, HS
Jewelweed or spotted jewelweed	*Impatiens capensis* or *I. pallida*	CE, M/GP, HS
Mexican milkweed	*Asclepias currasavica*	DW, PCN, PCC, HS
Mexican sunflower	*Tithonia rotundifolia* or *T. diversifolia*	CN, CE, M/GP, MW, PCN, PCC, HS
Nasturtium	*Tropaeolum tuberosum* or *T. speciosum*	CN, CE, M/GP, MW, PCN, PCC, HS
Penstemon, or beardtongue	*Penstemon* spp.	CN, CE, M/GP, MW, DW, PCN, PCC
Phlox	*Phlox* spp.	CN, CE, M/GP, MW, PCN, PCC, HS
Pineapple sage	*Salvia elegans*	CN, CE, M/GP, MW, DW, PCN, PCC, HS

ANNUALS AND PERENNIALS CONTINUED

COMMON NAME	SCIENTIFIC NAME	REGION
Red-hot poker, or tritoma	*Kniphofia uvaria*	CN, CE, M/GP, MW, PCN, PCC, HS
Scarlet gilia, or skyrocket	*Ipomopsis aggregata*	MW, DW, PCN, PCC
Scarlet sage, or red salvia	*Salvia splendens*	CN, CE, M/GP, MW, DW, PCN, PCC, HS
Snapdragon	*Antirrhinum majus*	CN, CE, M/GP, MW, PCN, PCC, HS
Spider flower	*Cleome spinosa*	CE, M/GP, MW, PCC, HS
Standing cypress	*Ipomopsis rubra*	CN, CE, M/GP, MW, DW, HS
Texas sage	*Salvia coccinea*	CN, CE, M/GP, MW, DW, PCC, HS
Zinnia	*Zinnia* spp.	CN, CE, M/GP, MW, DW, PCN, PCC, HS

VINES

COMMON NAME	SCIENTIFIC NAME	REGION
Coral, or trumpet, honeysuckle	*Lonicera sempervirens*	CN, CE, M/GP, MW, DW, PCC, HS
Cross vine	*Bignonia capreolata*	CE, M/GP, MW, HS
Cypress vine	*Ipomoea quamoclit*	CE, DW, PCC, HS
Firecracker vine	*Manettia cordifolia* or *M. inflata*	PCN, PCC, HS
Mexican flame vine	*Senecio confusus*	DW, PCC, HS
Red morning glory	*Ipomoea coccinea*	CE, MW, DW, HS
Scarlet runner bean	*Phaseolus coccineus*	CN, CE, M/GP, MW, DW, PCC, HS
Trumpet creeper	*Campsis radicans*	CN, CE, M/GP, MW, DW, PCN, PCC, HS

SHRUBS

COMMON NAME	SCIENTIFIC NAME	REGION
Azalea	*Rhododendron* spp.	CE, M/GP, PCN, HS
Beauty bush	*Kolkwitzia amabilis*	CN, CE, M/GP, MW, PCN, PCC
Bottlebrush	*Callistemon citrinus* or *C. speciosus*	DW, PCN, PCC, HS
Butterfly bush	*Buddleia alternifolia*	CN, CE, M/GP, MW, PCN, PCC, HS
Crimson-flowering currant	*Ribes sanguineum*	CE, M/GP, PCN, PCC
Flame acanthus	*Anisacanthus quadrifidus* var. *wrightii*	DW, PCC, HS
Flowering quince	*Chaenomeles speciosa*	CN, CE, M/GP, MW, DW, PCN, PCC, HS
Hardy fuchsia	*Fuchsia magellanica*	CN, CE, M/GP, MW, PCN, PCC
Hibiscus	*Hibiscus rosa-sinensis*	CE, M/GP, MW, PCN, PCC, HS
Lantana	*Lantana horrida* or *L. camara*	MW, DW, PCC, HS
Lilac	*Syringa vulgaris*	CE, M/GP, MW, PCN

COMMON NAME	SCIENTIFIC NAME	REGION
SHRUBS CONTINUED		
Manzanita	*Arctostaphylos* spp.	MW, DW, PCN, PCC
Red buckeye	*Aesculus pavia* var. *pavia*	CE, M/GP, MW, PCN, HS
Scarlet bush, or firebush	*Hamelia patens*	CE, M/GP, MW, DW, PCN, PCC, HS
Shrimp plant	*Justicia brandegeana*	DW, PCN, PCC, HS
Snowberry	*Symphoricarpus albus*	CN, CE, M/GP, MW, PCN, PCC
Sultan's turban	*Malvaviscus arboreus* var. *drummondii*	DW, PCC, HS
Turk's cap	*Malvaviscus arboreus* var. *mexicanus*	DW, PCC, HS
Weigela, or cardinal shrub	*Weigela florida*	CN, CE, M/GP, PCN, PCC, HS

COMMON NAME	SCIENTIFIC NAME	REGION
TREES		
Buckeye	*Aesculus glabra*	CN, CE, M/GP, HS
Black locust	*Robinia pseudoacacia*	CN, CE, M/GP, MW, PCN, PCC, HS
Citrus	*Citrus* spp.	DW, PCC, HS
Flowering crab apple	*Malus baccata* or *M. floribunda*	CN, CE, M/GP, MW, PCN, PCC, HS
Hawthorn	*Crataegus* spp.	CE, M/GP, DW, HS
Mimosa, or silk tree	*Albizia julibrissin*	CE, M/GP, PCN, PCC, HS
Red horse chestnut	*Aesculus hippocastanum* x *A. carnea*	CN, CE, M/GP, MW, PCN, HS
Siberian pea tree	*Caragana arborescens*	CN, CE, M/GP, MW, DW, PCN, PCC, HS
Tulip poplar	*Liriodendron tulipfera*	CN, CE, M/GP, MW, PCN, PCC, HS

We attract hummingbirds to our yards in two ways: by planting nectar-producing flowering plants and by offering a nectarlike solution in hummingbird feeders.

FLOWERS

Blooming flowers are the best attractant for hummingbirds. While the conventional wisdom has been that hummingbirds prefer red or orange flowers, I know from experience that "our" hummers visit flowers of all colors in our gardens.

Among the flowers that are popular with both gardeners and hungry hummingbirds are azaleas (*Rhododendron* spp.), bee balm (*Monarda* spp.), cardinal flower (*Lobelia cardinalia*), columbines (*Aquilegia* spp.), coralbells (*Heuchera sanguinea*), foxglove (*Digitalis* spp.), fuchsias (*Fuchsia* spp.), penstemon (*Penstemon* spp.), jewelweed (*Impatiens* spp.), larkspurs (*Delphinium* spp.), sages (*Salvia* spp.), and trumpet creeper (*Campsis radicans*).

The best hummingbird-friendly flowering plants for your region/climate/soil might vary, but these give you a starting point. In planning your hummingbird garden, choose plants that will bloom during different times of the growing season, so you'll always have some natural nectar available for your birds.

It's not just nectar the hummingbirds get from our flowering plants. They also eat aphids, gnats, and other small insects that live on and among the plants. Insects provide an important source of protein for hummingbirds.

In early spring, before most of our hummingbird plants are blooming, we "cheat" a little and put up some hanging baskets with fuchsias and impatiens that we've wintered over in our greenhouse. Before we had the greenhouse, we'd splurge for a hanging basket or two at our favorite garden center each spring. With these flowering plants out on the front porch, we knew we'd catch the eye of early-arriving migrants. Once we had them attracted, they would find our feeders, which would help keep them fed until our flower beds burst into bloom as the weather warmed.

WE USE POTTED PLANTS, *hanging flower baskets, and bird feeders to bring birds close to our kitchen windows, where we can enjoy them.*

FEEDERS

Birding lore tells us that the first person to feed a hummingbird was a young California girl who needed something to do while recovering from an illness. Noticing that the hummingbirds in her family's garden were visiting a certain type of flower, she picked a few and filled them with sugar water. She held these in her hands while sitting near the hummers' favorite flowering plants and, much to her delight, two male hummingbirds became her regular visitors. This happened in 1890! So you can see, backyard hummingbird feeding goes back quite a ways.

Hummingbird feeders are designed to deliver nectar to humming-birds, much as a tubular flower does. But unlike a single flower, which produces a finite amount of nectar each day, a feeder can deliver enough sugar water to supply dozens of birds.

There are hundreds of options available when you are purchasing a hummingbird feeder. There are a few key things to look for, however.

The feeder should have bright red parts to alert hummingbirds to its presence.

It should be easy to clean and fill. Feeders with ornate decorations and hard-to-reach nooks and crannies are hard to clean and refill.

It should have a nectar capacity that matches your volume of feeding. A feeder that is too small will need to be filled multiple times a day. A feeder that is too large will not be drained of nectar before the nectar goes bad.

In spring we start out with a small feeder or two, because the volume of birds visiting the feeder is low—perhaps just one or two early-returning males. Over the next few weeks, as the females return, the action at the feeders picks up and we add more and bigger feeders to our backyard. By late July, we're in full swing with adults and young swarming our high-capacity feeders.

NECTAR RECIPE

A sugar-water solution of 1 part white table sugar to 4 parts water most closely approximates the sucrose content of naturally occurring flower nectar. To make this nectar, boil 4 cups of water. Add 1 cup of sugar and stir until it is dissolved. Let it cool before pouring it into a hummingbird feeder. You can use any ratio of 4 to 1 (water to sugar) and refrigerate the excess for later use. Never use honey, molasses, artificial sweeteners, or artificial colors. White table sugar is the ingredient that most closely approximates natural flower nectar, when mixed in a 4-to-1 ratio. Resist the urge to mix stronger blends; sweeter is not better.

I know that our first hummingbird returns in the spring here in south-eastern Ohio about April 17. In anticipation of that major sign of spring, we have a few small hummingbird feeders cleaned, filled, and ready.

Over the years, we've settled on a few feeders that we use again and again. In general terms, these are models that permit many birds to feed at once. They are designed simply so they are easy to fill and clean. And *they don't drip or leak!* Ask at your local wild bird store for advice on the best feeders.

WHERE TO HANG FEEDERS

As with seed or suet feeders, the best place to hang your hummingbird feeders is where the birds can find them easily, where you can see them and access them easily, and out of direct sunlight to keep the nectar from growing yeast and mold (something the heat of the sun encourages).

MOLDY SOLUTION

Mold happens. Combine sugar with water and add a little heat—there's no way to avoid it. But by washing out your feeder every time you refill it, you can keep the mold at bay. We keep a special hummer-feeder cleaning brush near the kitchen sink all summer long. After filling the feeder with hot, soapy water, we scrub it out with the brush. We use special port-cleaning brushes to keep the feeding ports clear and clean. Any place we find a small bit of black scuzz growing on the feeder, we attack it. After the soap comes a good cleaning rinse with plain water, then a refill and rehanging. We often find the hummingbirds hovering in place, waiting for the feeder to return to its familiar spot.

RED DYE: WHY?

There has been much debate over the years about the addition of red dye in hummingbird solution. It's true that red attracts hummers. But it does not have to be in the form of dyed nectar. A red ribbon hanging from the feeder or red parts on the feeder itself will serve the same purpose. Red dye is completely unnecessary, so it's best to avoid it, whether you are making your own solution or buying solution mixtures at the store.

BULLIES: CLUMP YOUR FEEDERS!

If you have a hummingbird feeder, you will get an adult male that acts as though the feeder is his sole province. He will fight all other birds that attempt to visit the feeder, often crashing into them with a smack to drive them off. I used to recommend that the solution to this was to place other feeders around your yard, out of sight of your bully male. I found, however, that this only serves to permit other bully kingdoms to be set up.

Now I recommend that you group all of your feeders in a tight clump. In late summer, when adults and the young birds from the first brood are all trying to visit the feeders, your bullies will get tired and overwhelmed. Soon they will just give up and let everyone feed in peace.

Bluebirds

If you are lucky enough to have one or more of these lovely blue-colored thrushes visiting your property, you are the envy of bluebird-less bird watchers everywhere. We have eastern bluebirds on our farm year-round. In the spring and summer we watch them courting and nesting and feeding their young. In the winter we watch for their family foraging flocks to visit our meadow on sunny days and our suet-dough feeders when the weather gets bad.

SUET DOUGH *is an excellent high-energy winter food for many birds, like this male eastern bluebird.*

Eastern bluebirds are found in the East. Western and mountain bluebirds are found in the West. A few fortunate birders along the western edge of the Great Plains can see all three bluebirds. Being insect-eaters for most of the year, bluebirds are not naturally inclined to visit bird feeders. In fact, the best way to have a close relationship with bluebirds is to provide proper and safe nesting cavities for them in the form of bird houses (for more on housing for birds, see Chapter 5).

Our bluebirds were nearly wiped out during the middle of the twentieth century, thanks to the combined effects of increased pesticide use and increased competition for scarce nesting cavities from house sparrows and European starlings. A determined effort by a small number of bluebird enthusiasts forced the bluebirds' plight into the national spotlight. As a result, more North Americans began providing nest boxes for bluebirds and protecting their "tenants" from the dangers of weather, predators, and competitors. Today, the populations of all three species are healthy and even growing.

At our feeders bluebirds eat mealworms, suet dough, fruit, and sunflower bits. They also consume eggshell bits during spring and summer when the females need extra calcium for egg production.

MEALWORMS

Mealworms are not really worms. They are the larval form of a harmless, small black beetle. Feeding mealworms to wild birds has become a big trend in bird feeding. For insect-eaters, finding a bowl of squirmy, plump mealworms on an icy winter day is a food source that is too good to pass up. Bluebirds seem to *love* mealworms and will really key into your feeder if you offer them this specialty food. For more on mealworms, see page 25.

TOO MUCH OF A GOOD THING

As hard as it is to do, you need to refrain from feeding your birds as much of these high-protein, high-fat foods as they will eat. It can adversely affect their health and behavior. One summer, early in our mealworm-feeding days, we offered our front-yard bluebird pair all the mealies they could eat. They produced four large broods that summer, in response to the superabundant food source. By September, both parents looked ragged and worn—because they were! We felt really bad that we'd encouraged them to such extraordinary feats of reproduction, and we swore right then to be more careful. Now we offer only a small handful of mealworms or homemade suet dough in the morning, and perhaps a bit more in really bad weather when natural food is scarce.

This holds true for any high-protein or high-fat bird food, including suet and suet dough. You should not offer your birds too much of a good thing.

SUET DOUGH

We offer our favorite recipe for crumbly suet dough during winter and early spring. We feed in a similar fashion as with mealworms, offering one or two handfuls at a time in a dog dish. In winter we make suet dough in huge batches, and more than 20 species come in to eat it on a regular basis.

WE MAKE huge batches of suet dough in fall and winter, but we offer it in modest amounts to our birds. A dark-eyed junco and a field sparrow are among our many regulars at the suet-dough feeding spot.

SUET-DOUGH RECIPE

Ingredients

1 cup melted lard
1 cup peanut butter
2 cups quick oats
2 cups yellow cornmeal
1 cup all-purpose flour

Directions

Melt lard and peanut butter together in the microwave or on a low burner. Remove from heat and combine with dry ingredients. When cool, store in jars; no refrigeration needed. Offer crumbled in an open dish or packed into a suet log.

Winter Finches

When I was first getting really avid about bird watching, I was treated to a backyard phenomenon for two years in a row that I've never seen since: a winter finch invasion. The winters of 1977–1978 and 1978–1979 were *horrible* winters, with record-setting amounts of snow and cold temperatures. This coincided with a failure in the natural seed crop in the far North—the conifer and plant seeds that finches eat as their primary diet. So evening grosbeaks, common redpolls, pine siskins, purple finches (a nice change from our house finches), and both white-winged and red crossbills came south seeking food.

A COMMON REDPOLL (middle right) joins two pine siskins and an American goldfinch at a thistle feeder.

In backyards all across the upper half of the United States, these birds found feeders filled with sunflower seeds and thistle (now called Nyjer or niger seed). Bird feeding was taking off as a popular hobby, and seeds and feeders were starting to become more widely available commercially. In a sense, it was a perfect storm.

Our feeders on Warren Street in Marietta, Ohio, were mobbed with birds. We had a hard time keeping the feeders filled. Coincidentally, this was the year my family started *Bird Watcher's Digest,* so we thought this influx of unusual birds was a good omen.

In the 30 years since then, I've almost always maintained a set of bird feeders. And I've had a few nice little blasts of finches visiting my feeders, but never in the numbers and variety all at once that we had back in those two winters in the late 1970s.

Of the foods you normally offer at your bird feeders, the sunflower seeds and sunflower bits will be the most attractive to winter finches. If you don't already offer Nyjer seed to your goldfinches, you might want to consider adding it to your menu. It can be a bit more expensive than black-oil sunflower seed, and it requires a feeder with small holes to restrict the seed flow, but when finches such as redpolls, siskins, and—in the West—the rosy-finches key in to this food, you'll have them hooked for as long as they're around.

Evening grosbeaks prefer sunflower seed scattered on a large platform feeder. Given a choice, they seem to prefer striped sunflower seed to black oil, perhaps because their heavy seed-crushing bills can handle striped sunflower's harder shells.

Common and hoary redpolls, pine siskins, our goldfinch species, the rosy-finches, and purple, Cassin's, and house finches all readily consume black-oil sunflower seed and sunflower bits. They will use platform, hopper, and tube feeders, but they seem to prefer a feeder they can cling to while feeding.

The crossbills and pine grosbeak are less-regular feeder visitors than the other winter finches—they are more likely to come to your yard to pry the seeds out of pine, hemlock, and spruce cones. But they will visit bird feeders for sunflower seed if the activity of other finches draws their attention to the food source.

MORE BIRDS, MORE POOP

When a flock of winter finches descends on your feeding station, you'll have the extra work of keeping the fast-emptying feeders stocked. You'll also need to clean the feeders more regularly, because increased bird activity always means more bird poop. Flocks of birds feeding in close proximity create an ideal situation for the transmission of disease. When we get major action at our feeders, we not only clean the feeders more often (using bleach water to kill any pathogens), we also rake up the seed hulls from under the feeder when we can. If the ground is dry, I use my Shop-Vac to do the clean-up. If things are too wet and yucky, I move the feeding station to another part of the yard. This not only gets the birds away from the messy area, it gives the grass a chance to grow in that spot.

I keep hoping for another winter with redpolls and evening grosbeaks. It will happen some year. But with the increased popularity of bird feeding, I'm not sure the birds will make it all the way to southern Ohio. They might just find plenty to eat in the thousands of backyards they'll see before reaching mine.

Woodpeckers

At backyard feeding stations, woodpeckers may be among the most consistent patrons. The majority of our 23 North American woodpecker species (22 if you've given up hope for the ongoing existence of the ivory-billed woodpecker) will visit feeding stations at least occasionally.

Using their chisel-like bills, woodpeckers make quick work of suet or suet cakes, but they will also eat sunflower seeds and hearts, peanuts, peanut butter, cracked corn, and fruit. Some woodpeckers—especially red-bellieds, gilas, and golden-fronteds—will visit hummingbird feeders to drink nectar.

The woodpecker species that are our most common feeder visitors are the widespread downy and hairy woodpeckers. These two relatively small woodpeckers are found in a variety of habitats, from deep woodland and suburban backyards to urban parks. Both will join mixed-species feeding flocks in winter, roaming about with chickadees, titmice, nuthatches, kinglets, and others in search of food. When these flocks find a reliable source of food, such as a feeding station, it becomes a stop on their daily foraging route. In the Southwest, the closely related ladder-backed woodpecker is a fairly common visitor at bird feeders.

Red-bellied woodpeckers are feeder regulars throughout the eastern half of the United States and parts of southernmost Canada. They especially prefer cracked corn, suet, suet dough, and peanuts. In summer they can be attracted to orange halves impaled on tree-branch stubs.

Among the widespread woodpeckers that are less common at feeding stations are the northern flicker and the red-headed and pileated woodpeckers. Flickers do much of their foraging in an un-woodpecker-like way: they eat ants on the ground, poking their bill and long sticky tongue into anthills to extract their food. Both red-headeds and pileateds are more likely to be attracted to your trees than to your feeders, but some lucky backyard birders get pileateds to visit their large suet feeders,

SAPSUCKERS *drill holes in trees and return later to drink the sap the tree produces to protect itself. This is a juvenile yellow-bellied sapsucker.*

while others get red-headeds to come in to cracked corn, ears of field corn, or to peanuts offered on platform feeders.

Both red-headed woodpeckers and northern flickers are facultative migrants. This means they will migrate southward in winter only if necessary to find food and to avoid harsh weather. This seasonal movement probably also contributes to their inconsistency as feeder visitors. Our more steadfast woodpecker patrons are nonmigratory species.

In the West, we have a great variety of woodpeckers with ranges largely dictated by their habitat preferences. Within their somewhat constricted distribution, many of these species will visit feeding stations, though they are more likely to visit a yard if their preferred tree species and foods make the habitat sufficiently appealing. Traveling in the West, I always get a thrill watching acorn and Lewis's woodpeckers because they seem so much more colorful and animated than our eastern woodpeckers.

I should not neglect our four sapsucker species: red-naped, red-breasted, yellow-bellied, and Williamson's sapsuckers. These birds lap up—rather than suck—sap, using their short, bristle-ended tongue. To get this sap, sapsuckers drill small holes through the outer bark of certain tree species, causing the trees to emit protective sap. This sap contains sugar. The sapsuckers lick up the sap and also any insects attracted to it. Interestingly, other species of birds and animals will visit sapsucker sap wells, including several species of hummingbirds, warblers, other woodpeckers, and even squirrels and butterflies.

Of our four sapsucker species, only the yellow-bellied seems to be a regular feeder visitor. But even the yellow-bellieds will first be attracted to your yard by the presence of sap-rich trees, such as fruit trees, maples, and birches, among others.

Many backyard bird watchers find themselves purchasing specialized feeders for certain birds, and the woodpeckers are well represented in this trend. Thanks to their superior ability to cling while feeding, woodpeckers can use suet feeders that limit access to the underside of a feeder. These feeders are used primarily to foil hungry European starlings. There are also hanging suet and peanut feeders designed with extensions so that woodpeckers can use their stiff-feathered tails, which are specially adapted to support the birds as they cling and hitch up vertical tree branches.

It is especially gratifying on a cold winter day to watch our familiar woodpecker friends chisel off a piece of suet or a peanut kernel from the feeder, then swoop away in their undulating flight to consume the treat on a nearby tree.

Sparrows

Feeding sparrows is as easy as tossing a few handfuls of mixed seed on the ground, under the bushes, or along the edge of the patio. Nearly all of our sparrow species prefer to feed on or near the ground, so other than a low platform feeder, it's unlikely that you'll find them taking food out of a traditional bird feeder. (One exception is the ubiquitous and gluttonous house sparrow, which is a non-native species and not a sparrow at all, but a weaver finch.)

SONG SPARROWS spend much of their lives on or near the ground.

In actuality, you're much more likely to attract sparrows to your yard with good habitat. They prefer weedy edges, brambly hedgerows, vine tangles, and woodland edges. Even the foundation plantings of evergreen shrubs so common around office buildings and suburban homes are decent sparrow habitat. Once you've attracted sparrows with habitat, your feeder offerings can bring them into better view.

What is special about feeding sparrows is their subtle plumage and variety. Here on our farm in late fall and early winter, we often have song, chipping, field, white-throated, white-crowned, and fox sparrows at our feeders all at once. Add in the eastern towhees and dark-eyed juncos, two other members of the sparrow family, and we've got quite a nice mix of birds. Throughout the year we also get short visits from migrant swamp and Savannah sparrows, and we enjoy the winter company of a small flock of tree sparrows.

I dream of the day a Harris's sparrow will show up at our feeding station. Birders in the central United States, from Nebraska south to Texas, are the lucky hosts of this boldly marked sparrow. Along the Pacific Coast, another one of the "crowned" sparrows—the golden-crowned sparrow—visits feeders, scratching the ground for bits of seed.

Sparrows eat a variety of foods, from insects (available in season) to seeds, tree buds, fruits, and berries. Their somewhat conical bills show their close taxonomic relationship to the finches, but most sparrow bills lack the heavy seed-crushing ability that those of the finches possess. The sparrows' typical foraging style of scratching and sifting through leaves and duff to uncover food is taken to the extreme by the towhees and the fox sparrow. These larger sparrows sometimes get so enthusiastic in their scratching that it sounds like a much larger animal walking across the dead leaves. Numerous times I have followed that sound through the woods, expecting to see a large animal or perhaps a turkey, only to find a pair of eastern towhees intent on exposing things to eat below the fallen leaves.

The sparrows at your feeder will change with the seasons. This provides a backyard bird watcher with the chance to add to the yard list of bird species and also to work on the subtleties of sparrow identification.

Sparrow identification can be tricky. Some of us simply give up with a shrug, calling any small hard-to-ID sparrow an LBJ (for Little Brown Job).

SPARROW ID TIPS

As with any confusing bird, the best way to reach a correct identification is to be patient and methodical in your looking. First of all, make sure you are looking at a sparrow. Many nonbirders call any brown bird a sparrow. Our common sparrow species all have a short conical bill, round head, and fairly long tail. Start at the top of the sparrow's head and work your way down and back. Most birds in North America can be identified by their field marks from the shoulders up. Check for obvious patterns on the head and face, then move to the throat. Then look at the back of the neck, the shoulders, and the wings. Note the two or three most obvious field marks.

To make the most of your sparrow identification skills, look at the diagram of the parts of a bird in the front of your favorite field guide. It will help you learn the names and locations of some useful bird parts — many of which contain key field marks for our sparrows. Look at the various terms for the head: crown, forehead, malar, supercilium, eye-ring, eye line. These come in very handy in sparrow identification, along with some of the wing-related terms: shoulder, wing bars, scapulars, primaries, secondaries. It may sound daunting to learn these terms, but once you remember just a few of them, you'll be better prepared to note the important field marks on the sparrows at your feeder and in your yard.

Orioles and Other Fruit-eaters

It's a red-letter day when a bright male oriole flashes down from the treetops to visit the orange halves put out just for him. In my 30 years of feeding birds, I've been lucky enough to attract a Baltimore oriole to oranges only once. He stayed around for a few days, visiting the fruit in the morning, then he left for good. Our ridgetop farm does not yet have the tall deciduous trees this species prefers for nesting, so the stunning male oriole I nicknamed Cal Ripken left us to seek better habitat elsewhere.

We have five oriole species in North America, north of Mexico, that enjoy widespread distribution. In the East, the Baltimore oriole is joined by the orchard oriole. In the West, the Bullock's oriole (a close relative of the Baltimore) is the most widely distributed, followed by the Scott's oriole and hooded oriole with ranges restricted to the Southwest. All of these birds will visit backyards for fruit or nectar at hummingbird feeders, or for access to a regular source of water.

It's our birdbath that's gotten us our closest encounters with Baltimore and orchard orioles. They may not nest in our yard (yet!), but our large shallow basin with moving water is a must-stop for the orioles in late summer.

A MALE BALTIMORE ORIOLE eats from a halved orange during spring migration.

Fruit feeders are available commercially, but you can also create your own quite easily. The simplest way is to impale an orange or grapefruit half on the broken stub of a tree branch. Anything on which you can impale a piece of fruit will do. Our old feeder pole featured a pair of dowels I'd stuck into drilled holes. I angled them upward and sharpened them slightly on the exposed end to aid in the impaling.

We also offer old grapes, melon rinds, raisins, apple chunks, bananas, and other fruit on our platform feeder. Other birds will consume the fruit you offer at your feeders as well. We've had some surprising visitors: brown thrashers, a northern mockingbird, red-bellied woodpeckers, nuthatches, and even a ruby-throated hummingbird that was catching the fruit flies off the old bananas we put out.

One caveat: if you have fruit-loving mammals that visit your feeders at night, you may wish to offer your fruit in a way that keeps it out of their reach. We have raccoon problems at our feeders, but I have friends who have a bigger feeder pest: black bears. I'll talk more about feeder-visitor problems in Chapter 7. For now, let's look at some smaller furry feeder regulars: the squirrels.

Squirrels

I'm going to make a gross generalization here: most people who operate bird feeders don't like to let squirrels pig out there, too. Why? Because squirrels not only keep the birds away, they also eat everything they can. And if they can't get at the food inside a wooden or plastic feeder, they'll chew it open.

If you are a squirrel lover, I apologize. I'll even throw in some squirrel-feeding advice: they love whole ears of field corn. Buy a special squirrel feeder for them and let them eat until they can barely waddle back to their trees.

My parents have bad squirrel problems at their feeders in a small-town backyard. It took my dad years to find a set of squirrel-resistant feeders and pole baffles that worked to keep the squirrels from eating every sunflower seed in his tube feeder. That lasted about four days. Then the squirrels figured out how to jump from the tree to the garage roof, then down onto the feeder—rendering the baffle below the feeder completely useless. Trapping and removing the squirrels is illegal, dangerous, and morally suspect. Besides, all you'd be doing is removing the healthiest, most dominant squirrels from the scene.

They will be replaced by weaker, less-healthy squirrels. Shooting the squirrels is also illegal in most areas—and not for the faint-of-heart. I don't recommend it.

No, the best way to win the squirrel war is to make them your friends. Feed them exactly what they want, in moderate amounts but enough to hold their attention, far away from your bird feeders.

Walk down the aisle of any specialty wild bird store and you'll see that defeating squirrels has become a million-dollar-a-year industry. There are dozens of feeders designed to exclude, toss, shock, scare, flip, drop, and otherwise discourage squirrels from visiting. Some are packaged with cute and funny graphics of bandito squirrels. Others market themselves as "The *only* squirrel-proof feeder you'll ever need!" Most of this is unbelievable hype. If a squirrel can get to your feeder, it can get to the seed. If it can get to the seed, your only hope is to give it food elsewhere (try the other end of the yard), where the furry menace does not have to work so hard.

When we moved to our farm in southeastern Ohio, we had a neighbor who adorned the antenna of his truck with the tails of the squirrels he shot in his woods and ate. Little did we know, he also hunted in our woods. We never had a squirrel problem at our feeders. Well, that neighbor died a few years back. Yesterday I saw two huge gray squirrels looking at our feeders from the edge of our woods and licking their furry chops.

It looks like I'm going back into battle. Let the squirrel wars begin!

Chapter 7 Trouble in Paradise

AT SOME POINT IN YOUR BIRD FEEDING you will face some challenges, problems, and frustrations. During my two-plus decades as an editor of *Bird Watcher's Digest,* I've been asked a *lot* of bird questions—by our subscribers, by my fellow bird watchers, and by folks who don't know the difference between a cardinal and a Cooper's hawk. Many of these questions have made it into the old FAQ file (a folder I keep of Frequently Asked Questions).

Here are the most commonly asked of the FAQs, divided up into logical (I hope) categories.

Hummingbirds
MIGRATION AND FEEDERS

Q: *Is it true that hummingbirds at my feeder will not migrate if I leave my feeder up in the fall?*

A: No. This is another in a long line of bird myths. Birds are genetically programmed to migrate when their internal "clocks" tell them to do so. They will depart when the time is right, whether your feeders are up or not. Leaving your feeders up in the fall, however, and getting them up early in the spring may help late or early migrants that are passing through your area.

HUMMINGBIRD FEEDERS *with perches allow multiple birds to share a feeder. These are Anna's hummingbirds of varying ages. Adult males show the magenta throat and crown; adult females show a small magenta throat patch, and juveniles have a plain throat.*

AGGRESSIVE HUMMERS

Q: *How do I foil a "bully" hummer?*

A: Many hummingbird species defend feeding territories, and assemblages at feeders usually develop hierarchies. The behavior exemplifies natural selection at work, and you should do nothing except enjoy it. If you're worried about hungry hummers, put up several more feeders near the original one. The bully will be overwhelmed by sheer numbers of other birds and will be less territorial.

ANTS AND BEES

Q: *How do I keep ants and bees out of the hummingbird feeder?*

A: Select a hummingbird feeder with bee guards, which prevent bees and yellowjackets from drinking, and replace feeders that drip. You can discourage ants from getting to your hummer food by painting laundry detergent on the surface the ants use to reach the feeder (don't paint the feeder). The solution interferes with the ants' chemical navigation. Refresh the application several times the first day. After a few days, you won't need it anymore.

Bird Problems

WINDOW STRIKES

Q: *How can I keep birds from flying into my windows?*

A: Silhouettes of flying hawks or falcons do work, but they perform best when applied on the outside of the glass. A series of feathers strung along a piece of fishing line and hung across the outside surface seems to be an effective deterrent. Hanging ornaments such as wind chimes, windsocks, and potted plants in front of windows also helps. Misting the outside of the window with a very weak detergent or soda solution will eliminate the reflection but will also impair visibility for you. Awnings, eave extensions, and window screens will eliminate all reflection and stop the collision problem. Plastic cling wrap applied to the inside or outside of the window can also be effective.

Another solution is to move your feeders within 3 feet of windows that get frequent bird strikes. This won't prevent strikes, but it will decrease the speed at which any birds hit, because they cannot reach full flying speed across such a short distance.

Still another technique is to make a window covering of crop netting. We recently constructed a crop-netting covering for a series of three large windows in our house. These windows seem to attract bird strikes, especially on overcast days. We had tried every deterrent, but the sheer size of the windows made it impossible to make the windows strike-proof. We also tried placing window screens over the outside of the windows but found that they cut our visibility too much and blocked too much light. The crop netting is easy to see through, does not cut out light, and makes it physically impossible for birds to hit our windows. The netting is strung across a series of rectangular frames that outline each window. The frames are made of PVC pipe, painted to match our window-trim color. Metal shelf brackets hold the frames in place about 10 inches out from the windows. Thus far we've had only a few birds hit the netting. All of them bounced backward lightly and flew off in another direction. We no longer hear that sickening thud of a bird striking our windows, and it's a great relief.

HIGHLIGHTER LINES REDUCE WINDOW STRIKES

An intriguing window-strike deterrent involves drawing lines on your windows with a bright yellow highlighter. Birds can see portions of the ultraviolet light spectrum that human eyes cannot. Birder David Sibley conducted experiments on his problem windows in Massachusetts and determined that a grid of lines drawn with a yellow highlighter on the inside of the glass pane helped reduce window strikes, apparently by making the glass more noticeable to birds. The birds saw the grid lines and did not fly into the glass. This partial solution does require regular redrawing of the lines, which fade in direct sunlight. And it is not 100 percent effective in stopping all collisions—only a mesh net screen over the windows can accomplish that.

BIRD REFLECTIONS

Q: *We have a cardinal that has declared war on our house. He starts whacking himself into our windows at 6:00 A.M. and will not quit until the sun goes down. How long will this behavior last?*

A: The behavior will last through the breeding season. In some individuals it may go on year-round, for years. It's a territorial reaction to seeing an intruder on its "turf." Covering the windows with screens will help, but the bird may just move to another window. You might try screening or plastic wrap on the outside surfaces of the window. Remove any perches from which the bird can see itself in the windows. And continue to harass the bird, to try to shock it out of its pattern of territoriality. (Spraying the bird with the garden hose may work, and rubber snakes hung by the windows sometimes do the trick.) If all else fails, call your local wildlife officials and ask them to come out and remove the bird for you. It's drastic, but it will end the problem.

WOODPECKERS ON SIDING

Q: *I have a woodpecker that is pecking holes in my house siding. Is there anything I can do to get him to stop?*

A: A woodpecker drilling on your wooden house is only doing what comes naturally to it—drilling into wood in search of shelter or food. Most house-wrecking woodpeckers do their damage in the fall, which is when they begin making their winter roost holes. Try mounting a nest box with an appropriately sized hole over the drilled area. Fill the box with woodchips, and you may divert the bird's attention and gain a tenant. In spring, woodpeckers also use wood and sometimes metal parts of houses as drumming sites to announce their territory and attract a mate. There are several things you can try.

- Place some sheet metal or heavy aluminum foil over the area the bird is using.
- Hang some aluminum pie plates around the affected area. Make sure they move in the wind, to scare the bird.
- Place a rubber snake near the drilling area.
- Repeatedly scare the bird when it lands on your house.
- If nothing else works, call your local wildlife official, who may come to your house to remove the offending bird.

SNAKES AND BIRDS

Q: *A snake ate my bluebirds right out of the box. How can I prevent this?*

A: Pole-mounted baffles are the only way to keep snakes and most other predators from getting to a box full of bluebirds. Unbaffled boxes mounted on fenceposts or trees offer no protection against natural predators. For more on baffles, see page 70.

BLACK SNAKES *are frequent predators of bird nests.*

HEADLESS BIRDS

Q: *I keep finding decapitated birds in my yard. What's doing it?*

A: In urban and suburban settings, grackles are the most likely culprits, although jays, magpies, and crows will also decapitate small birds. Screech-owls and pygmy-owls also decapitate their prey, but intending to eat them later, they usually cache their victims out of sight.

NOCTURNAL BIRD SONG

Q: *Every spring I have a bird that sings not only throughout the day but all night long. I love the sound of birds, but this drives me nuts! This bird has many different songs. What is it, and what can I do about it?*

A: Your bird is most likely a northern mockingbird. Don't worry, male mockingbirds perform this nocturnal singing only in spring, during a full moon. I suggest running an electric fan (to create a sound buffer) and using your earplugs on nights when the mockingbird is singing. Having a mocker around is a good thing—you might even consider yourself lucky!

Predators and Pests

STOPPING STARLINGS

Q: *What kind of feeder will discourage starlings?*

A: Tube feeders seem to work best at making life difficult for starlings. This species is incredibly adaptable. You may want to stop feeding peanuts, mixed seed, bread products, table scraps, and suet for a few days to discourage starlings. Try limiting your feeding to black-oil sunflower seed.

EUROPEAN STARLINGS may mob feeding stations during periods of inclement weather, temporarily chasing off other birds.

PIGEON PROBLEMS

Q: *How do I get rid of pigeons without harming blue jays, cardinals, grackles, woodpeckers, and squirrels?*

A: City pigeons, or rock pigeons (formerly called rock doves), can be a plague at some urban and suburban feeding stations, where they dominate the feeders and gobble up all the food. Here are a few techniques for discouraging them.

ROCK PIGEONS *(also called rock doves or feral pigeons) can be messy feeder visitors. They thrive equally well in urban settings and rural farmyards.*

- Watch what they eat and quit serving it until they stop visiting.
- Don't put feed on the ground, ledges, platforms, or any flat surfaces. Use only hanging feeders that sway and feeders that are too small for the rock pigeons.
- Keep all excess food cleaned up off the ground.
- Lure the rock pigeons away from your main feeding area by putting their preferred food someplace where you can tolerate them.
- Discourage these birds from roosting nearby by using chickenwire to screen off roosting sites.

FOILING SPARROWS

Q: *House sparrows have learned how to get into my suet block. They hang from the bottom of the wire-caged, top-covered, hanging block just like chickadees. Any suggestions for keeping this food source away from the sparrows but available to the less-aggressive species?*

A: Three combined actions might help: First, insert a spring in the line from which you hang the suet block. It should be tighter than a Slinky but flexible enough to allow some bobbing action triggered by the weight of a small bird. Swinging and twisting motions combined with up-and-down motion usually discourage everything except downy woodpeckers, chickadees, siskins, and goldfinches.

Second, hang more than one suet block. Decoy house sparrows away from your main feeding area with a stationary suet block close to the ground.

Third, reduce the number of house sparrows in your neighborhood by eliminating access to protected nesting sites. Watch the sparrows in spring, and they'll show you where those sites are. In extreme cases, sparrow traps such as those sold

HOUSE SPARROWS are non-native birds that compete fiercely for nest sites with native cavity-nesting songbirds such as bluebirds, swallows, woodpeckers, chickadees, and titmice.

by the Purple Martin Conservation Association and the North American Bluebird Association can be used to live-trap house sparrows. See the Resources section at the back of this book for contact information.

Q: *What can I do to limit the number of sparrows at my feeders?*

A: Here are a few tips for reducing house sparrows at your feeders.

- Stop feeding mixed seed and cracked corn.
- Reduce ground feeding.
- Use tube feeders with perches.
- Feed only black-oil sunflower seed.

FOILING BLACKBIRDS

Q: *Red-winged blackbirds and grackles have taken over my feeders. My feeders are kind of large. Should I change to smaller feeders, or is there a better method?*

A: Your best bet is to switch to tube feeders and to eliminate feeding on the ground. Feed only black-oil sunflower seed for the time being—no mixed seed or cracked corn. Blackbirds at feeders are largely a fall and winter phenomenon. Once spring migration starts, the large blackbird flocks start to break up and head north.

Q: *I read that starlings, blackbirds, and grackles do not like safflower seeds but that smaller birds (titmice, chickadees) do. Is this true? And if so, will it keep*

BLACKBIRDS form large foraging and roosting flocks in fall and winter. They are often part of mixed-species flocks that may also contain grackles, blackbirds, and cowbirds.

the larger birds from cleaning out our feeders before the smaller ones can get to them?

A: Some blackbirds will eat safflower only when there's nothing else to eat. Cardinals seem to love it. If you want to feed smaller birds, get small roofed feeders that exclude the larger birds (globe feeders and domed feeders work well). These feeders have adjustable roofs that prevent larger birds from accessing the food.

HAWKS AT FEEDERS

Q: *How can I discourage the hawk that has been stalking my feeders?*

A: Accipiters (Cooper's and sharp-shinned hawks are two) are bird-eating hawks that commonly visit feeding stations. You can't prevent these predators from hunting in your yard, but here are some things you can do to encourage them to look for easier meals elsewhere.

- Create shelter and escape habitat for the feeder birds, using shrubs, trees, brush piles, and brushy areas.
- Move your feeders from the middle of an open area and create a brush pile nearby so it's harder for a hawk to surprise and catch birds.
- Quit feeding for a time to encourage all birds to disperse.

CATS AND BIRDS

Q: *What can I do to protect the birds in my yard from cats?*

A: Hang feeders at least 5 feet above the ground. For ground-feeding birds, arrange ornamental border fencing in two or three concentric circles about 16 inches to 2 feet apart, to disrupt a cat's ability to leap at feeders or to spring on birds. Harass offending cats with a spray of water to train them to avoid your yard. I've found that white vinegar in a Super Soaker squirt gun is very effective. It dismays the cat, which cannot lick the vinegar off—something it will always associate with being in your yard. If all else fails, use a live trap to catch the cats and take them to the local animal shelter. If the cats belong to your neighbors, ask them to restrain their pets from accessing your yard. Check with your local animal control officer to see what legal options are available to you.

ACCIPITERS *visit bird-filled backyards looking for a meal. This sharp-shinned hawk is watching our feeders like . . . well, like a hawk. The feeder birds are motionless, waiting for the hawk to go away.*

KEEPING SQUIRRELS *off your feeders is a baffling problem — literally.*

STOPPING SQUIRRELS

Q: *I've read that putting hot pepper powder in birdseed prevents squirrels from eating the seed. Doesn't this harm the birds?*

A: Some birds naturally eat chili peppers in the wild. The chemical capsaicin in chili peppers or chili powder is what our human pain receptors sense as heat from the chili. Mammals are far more sensitive to this than birds. Research suggests that bird's pain receptors are largely insensitive to capsaicin. Pepper-laced seed may discourage squirrels, but it will not hurt birds in the same way.

However, let's not forget that we humans are sensitive to hot pepper. If you use one of the various pepper-seed additives, be very careful and wash your hands thoroughly after touching the seed.

Q: *How do I keep squirrels off my bird feeders?*

A: Baffling your feeders is the best way to prevent squirrels from gaining access to them. Hang the feeder from a thin wire, far from any object from which the squirrels can leap. String the wire with empty water bottles, which spin and dump the squirrels off. There are many squirrel-proof feeders on the market that may give the squirrels a small electric shock or that rotate or bounce to dump the squirrels off. But be forewarned: squirrels have been known to outsmart the most ingenious of squirrel-proof inventions.

If you can't beat 'em, join 'em. Feed squirrels ears of dried corn, but place the corn away from your bird feeders. Given the choice, squirrels will always go for the easiest food, and they love corn.

SEED AND SUET PESTS

Q: *The black-oil sunflower seeds in my 50-pound bag have tiny holes in them, and I've observed moths emerging from the seed shells. What causes this, and how can I prevent it from happening again?*

A: The seed-drilling culprit is a weevil that lays its eggs on developing sunflower seeds. The hatching larvae consume the kernel and then drill exit holes through the shells.

Sunflower farmers constantly wage war against sunflower weevils, but despite their best efforts, infested seeds occasionally survive harvesting and processing. A seed's weight may indicate

if it is contaminated. This is why a chickadee picks up and discards many seeds before selecting one and flying away. The bird is searching for a healthy seed with the largest nutmeat, rather than one that is lighter and potentially weevil-infested.

The moths you've noticed are probably Indian meal moths or adult sunflower weevils that have drilled through the seed shells. The meal moths can be controlled using pheromone-based meal moth traps, which are available in garden and hardware stores.

Storing the seed in airtight containers keeps the contents fresh and controls pests. We pour our 50-pound bags into large plastic or metal garbage cans with tight-fitting lids. I've also successfully deterred insect infestations by placing several large bay leaves in my sunflower seed.

If your seed is infested with weevils, throw it out and buy a new bag. If you purchase seed at a reputable retail store and experience weevil problems, tell the store owner or manager. He or she should offer to replace your seed, or at least check into the shipment involved.

AMONG the most trouble-some feeder visitors are raccoons. Raccoons will empty the food from feeders and may even steal feeders that are not wired in place.

Q: *Who or what is stealing my suet?*

A: Crows, cats, bears, skunks, squirrels, raccoons, foxes, weasels, dogs, coyotes, and even some hawks and owls could be responsible for the missing suet.

I suggest you suspend the feeder on a wire from your eaves, a pole, or a handy tree branch. Hang it high enough so a leaping cat or dog can't reach it, but close enough for you to access for refilling. And take a few peeks during the night—you might catch your suet thief in the act!

Sick, Injured, and Dead Birds

Q: *What do I do with the sick bird at my feeders? What's wrong with it?*

A: Any busy backyard feeding station will have its share of unhealthy birds. They are the last ones to fly away when you approach to fill the feeders. And they are often the birds that are captured and eaten by predators such as sharp-shinned or Cooper's hawks. One of the downsides to operating a feeding station is that it can become a vector for disease if not regularly cleaned and disinfected. The concentration of birds in a small area naturally leads to an accumulation of seed hulls and bird droppings. A visit by one sick bird can spread illness to others.

If you see a sick bird, it's best to stop feeding for a few days to allow the healthy birds to disperse. Take down your feeders and wash them in a hot bleach-water solution (1 part bleach to 9 parts water). Rinse with plain water and let them dry. It's important to do this at least once a month during periods of heavy feeder activity—more often if needed. I also move our feeding station at least once a year. This gives the ground below the old feeding site a chance to recover, and it gets the birds away from the mess.

I know it seems like a lot of work, but it sure beats finding sick or dead birds below your feeders.

If you find a sick bird, it's best to leave it alone. Sick birds are often lethargic, and they may show puffed-out plumage, drooping wings, swollen eyes, or other physical symptoms. If a bird is sick or diseased, there is little you or a licensed rehabilitator can do for it. So it is best to let nature take its course.

If you find a dead bird near your feeders, put on some rubber gloves or other hand protection (plastic bags work too) and dispose of the bird in the trash or by burying it in the ground. While there is little chance of transmission of disease from bird to human, there's no point taking a chance.

If a bird has struck a window and is stunned or has been injured by a cat, place it in a paper bag folded closed or in a box with a lid. Close the container and leave the bird in a warm, safe, quiet place. Over the next hour or more, it may recover enough to be released. If it is badly injured but seems otherwise alert, contact a licensed bird rehabilitator in your area for advice. You can find one via the Internet or through your local wildlife officer.

BALD CARDINALS

Q: *I have two bald cardinals at my feeders. Why are they bald? Is it something I'm feeding?*

A: Your cardinals are probably victims of skin-burrowing avian feather mites that eat the feathers and cause the birds to "go bald." The mites exist on the birds in the only place the birds cannot preen themselves—the head. In a month or so you should have no bald cardinals, because the birds will have molted in a new set of feathers. The mites are perfectly natural, not caused by diet, and relatively harmless, unless the bird is in an otherwise weakened state.

A BALD CARDINAL is a common sight in late summer, when feather-mite infestations may consume a cardinal's head feathers. The head is the only place a bird cannot preen these pests away. Bald birds grow a new set of head feathers within a few weeks.

DEFORMED BILLS

Q: *What causes deformed bills on birds? A mourning dove with an odd-looking bill comes to my feeder.*

A: Deformities can be caused by several factors, including injury, natural genetic mutation, genetic inbreeding, and exposure to certain chemicals during embryonic development. In short, even if all the dioxin, PCBs, and DDT-like pesticides disappeared, birds would still occasionally appear with deformed bills.

INJURED BIRDS

Q: *I found an injured bird. What should I do with it?*

A: Special permits from the federal, state, or provincial government are required to handle injured or dead nongame bird species. Whereas your first instinct may be to call your local veterinarian, many are unwilling to care for wildlife cases. Often the best thing to do is nothing at all. As part of nature's cycle of life and death, an injured or dead bird may be a meal for another animal. If you feel you must do something to help an injured bird, call your local wildlife office or fish and game or extension office, which may know of a licensed rehabilitator in your area. See the Resources section at the end of this book.

SICK HOUSE FINCHES

Q: *I have seen two house finches with swollen red eyes at my feeder. They don't seem to be able to see very well, and they don't fly away when I get near them. What is wrong with them?*

A: It sounds like the birds may be suffering from house finch disease (Mycoplasmal conjunctivitis). House finches are not the only birds to get the disease, but it spreads more rapidly among them because they tend to flock at feeders more than some other birds.

Take down your feeders and clean them with a 10 percent bleach solution (1 part bleach and 9 parts water). Let them dry completely and then rehang them. Rake underneath the feeder to remove old seed and bird droppings.

FALLEN NESTLINGS

Q: *If I find a young bird that has fallen from a nest, what should I do?*

A: Try to place the nestling back in its nest if at all possible. This will be the young bird's best chance for survival. If you can't find the nest or a place to put the nestling out of harm's way, you will need to get the bird to a licensed rehabilitator as soon as possible. Baby birds are unable to thermoregulate (regulate their body temperature), so they must be kept in a protected area with a heat source. A soft nest made of tissues inside a small cardboard box, placed on a heating pad set on low, is a good temporary home. A moist sponge placed in the box will add a touch of desired humidity.

Your state or provincial fish and wildlife officers are responsible for licensing and regulating the activities of rehabilitators and have listings for all rehabbers in your state.

If a fledgling is found hopping around on the ground, it should be left alone if it's in a safe area. It can be placed up on a tree branch or in a shrub if it's in a dangerous situation, but it must remain in the same area so that its parents can find it. Young birds often leave the nest before they are capable of flight. They spend a few pre-flight days hopping on the ground and flapping their wings. Its parents are keeping an eye on it and feeding it when necessary. During this time the fledgling is learning valuable survival lessons from its parents.

THE BEST THING TO DO if you find a fledgling bird is to leave it alone. Many fledglings, such as this young northern cardinal, are well adapted to survive after leaving the nest, despite their downy, flightless appearance.

EMERGENCY FOOD FOR NESTLINGS

Q: *What do I feed to an orphaned baby bird?*

A: If you find an orphaned nestling songbird and there's no licensed rehabilitator immediately available to receive the youngster, here is a recipe for basic baby bird care.

Grind up dry dog food into a powder. Add warm water to make a yogurtlike slurry. Offer it to the bird through a baby medicine syringe, gently prying the bill open. Keep the bird warm in a tissue nest inside a box. If necessary, use a warm water bottle or heating pad on low placed nearby. Get the bird to a wildlife rehabilitator as soon as possible.

DEAD CROWS

Q: *We found two dead crows in the street in front of our house. What killed them?*

A: If you found the birds in the road, they were most likely killed by cars while eating roadkill—perhaps they were young, inexperienced birds. However, there is reason to be careful around dead crows. In recent years American crows have been dying from West Nile virus. If you find any more dead crows, call your local wildlife officials and have the crows tested for this disease. West Nile can be transmitted to humans but only via mosquito bite. Contact your local health department for information about any occurrence of West Nile in your area.

No Feeder Visitors

Q: *I've just put out new bird feeders, but no birds are visiting. Why not?*

A: One of the most frustrating things experienced by brand-new backyard bird watchers is that there are no birds visiting their brand-new bird feeders. Let's say you've spent $100 on fancy bird feeders and all the proper foods. You've placed the feeders just so, right outside the family-room window. Oh, the excitement! The anticipation! You skip back inside, grab a cup of tea, settle into your easy chair ready to be entertained, and . . . nothing. Your feeders just sit there, filled to the brim, with only the sun and a light breeze as visitors. What's worse is that this continues for two weeks!

What did you do wrong? Nothing.

It can take birds a long time to discover that those shiny contraptions hanging in your yard are full of delicious and nutritious bird food. Once they do discover this treasure trove of edibles, they will tell all of their friends and your feeders will be hopping.

FINDING FOOD AND FEEDERS

Q: *How do birds find new feeding stations? One bird appears, then more individuals of the same species, and soon other species appear. How does the word get spread?*

A: Birds are highly mobile creatures, adapted to finding and taking advantage of changing food supplies. Studies have shown that birds use vocal and visual clues to locate food. For example, a bird flying over an area of great activity, such as a feeding station, will be attracted by the noise and movements of the birds feeding below. Flocking species, such as finches and blackbirds, may be alerted to a food source by one individual. In winter, many small woodland species such as chickadees, nuthatches, kinglets, woodpeckers, and creepers form loose-knit feeding flocks that range about, benefiting from the extra eyes a flock provides in locating food and spotting predators.

Chapter 8
How to Identify a Bird

Identifying Backyard Birds

WE'VE ALL HAD THE EXPERIENCE of seeing an unfamiliar bird at a feeder or in our yard. At first there's a rush of excitement: Hey! There's a new bird! What is it? Sometimes this excitement turns to frustration when we aren't immediately able to identify the bird. And if the unidentified bird becomes an unidentified flying object and leaves, never to return, well, let's just say there have been a few uncivilized words spoken in my house when a bird gets away unidentified.

How do you avoid (or at least reduce) these frustrating situations? You practice your backyard bird identification skills by—get this— watching the birds at your feeder more often and more closely. Do you think you can handle that?

Here are a few tips to help you on the path to backyard bird ID enlightenment.

1. Watch the birds in your yard or at your feeders as often as you can. Even five minutes more watching per day will increase your familiarity with your regular visitors. Then, when something unusual shows up, it will stand out to your trained eyes immediately.

2. Look at the bird, not at the book. We bird watchers have a tendency to rely too heavily on our field guides to help us solve ID riddles. We may take a quick glance at the bird, note one obvious thing about it (it's yellow!), and then drop our binoculars and reach for the guide for the answer (there are *dozens* of yellow birds in the field guide). Needing more info, we drop the guide, raise our binocs, and look for the . . . it's gone! Birds have wings, books don't. Look at the bird for as long as you can. Go for the guide only once you've established a solid visual involving more than one field mark. Ideally, you'll note the three most obvious things about the bird before you look at the guide.

3. Start at the top, or front, of the bird (the end with the head and bill) and work your way down and back (toward the tail end), noting the three most obvious field marks.

4. Take some notes to help you remember. My mind is not what it used to be. It's not old age as much as it is a lack of space in my brain. There is so much "stuff" that we carry around in our heads these days, it's a wonder we can remember to keep blinking our eyes and breathing. Taking a few notes about an unfamiliar bird—especially if your field guide is not handy—can be the difference between an unsolved mystery and a clinched ID.

5. Assume it's something common, at least at first. Bald cardinals, baby towhees, summer starlings, baby cowbirds, and albino and leucistic (partly white) birds are the subject of about 75 percent of the bird identification calls we get at our office. Before presuming you've got a bird at your feeder that's new to science, look at it carefully and see if it doesn't remind you of one of your familiar visitors. Or perhaps it's associating with other, more normal-looking individuals of its species. Once you've ruled out the common birds, it's time to call in some help.

6. Report unusual sightings to your friends and the local birding network. If you've been birding for a while, you surely know others who share your fascination and hobby. These are the first friends to call to get a second opinion. If they agree that your bird is something unusual, call your local birding experts. Someone will be happy to look at photos you send, or maybe even to come over for a look-see themselves. Every so often—several times a year in North America—a really rare or unusual bird shows up at a feeder or in a backyard, and it sets the birding hotlines and e-mail group lists on fire with excitement.

7. Have fun. After all, that's why we watch birds, isn't it?

The species I've included in this final section of the book are birds that regularly show up at bird feeders and birdbaths and in backyards and gardens. A few (like the turkey vulture) merely *fly over* these same places, but they are commonly encountered nonetheless.

Each species profile includes information describing that bird, its field marks, sounds, habitat preferences, and what foods and features may attract it to your yard. One or two photographs accompany each profile, but some of the individuals you encounter may appear slightly different because of the effects of molting, age, weather, and light conditions. The birds in this guide are listed in taxonomic order, which is the organization ornithologists and other scientists use to group related bird species and families. Most other bird guides are also based on taxonomic order.

This backyard bird field guide is a starting place for you, no matter where in North America you live. The range maps are intended to help you sort out which species are likely to be seen in your part of the continent. But since birds don't read our maps, you may occasionally see a bird that is uncommon in your area, so keep an open mind.

If you wish to venture beyond the species that are included here, and perhaps even to venture beyond your backyard to see other birds (and I hope you will), you'll want to purchase one of the many excellent field guides available at your local bookstore. A list of these guides appears in the Resources section at the end of this book.

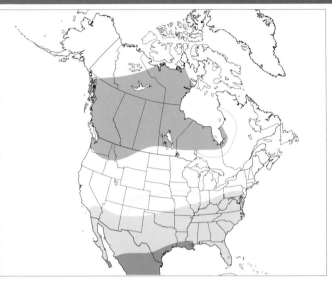

Key to Range Maps

- ☐ **Red:** summer range
- ☐ **Blue:** winter range
- ☐ **Purple:** year-round range
- ⋯⋯ **Red dash line:** approximate limits of irregular summer range and/or post-breeding dispersal
- ⋯⋯ **Blue dash line:** approximate limits of irregular winter range
- ⋯⋯ **Purple dash line:** approximate limits of irregular year-round range

Wood Duck

Aix sponsa   SIZE: 19"

The wood duck may be the most beautifully colored waterfowl species in North America. It is named for its habit of perching and nesting in trees. In the past half-century the wood duck population has recovered greatly from overhunting, thanks to the placement of nesting boxes in swampy habitat.

FIELD MARKS
The ornately colored male is distinctive: crested green head, red eye, orange bill, white throat, plum-colored breast and undertail, buffy yellow sides, and iridescent back. Females are drab by comparison but have teardrop-shaped white spectacles around the eyes.

SOUNDS
The male's call is a hissing, rising *jeee-eeb!* The female's flight call is an *ooeeeek!*

HABITAT
Wooded swamps, rivers, ponds, and marshes. May nest in tree cavities far from water.

BACKYARD
If you have a large backyard pond, you can offer nest boxes for this species.

Wood Ducks: female (left) and male

Plain Chachalaca

Ortalis vetula   SIZE: 22"

The only member of the currasow and guan family to reach the United States, the plain chachalaca is a year-round resident of the Rio Grande Valley in south Texas.

FIELD MARKS

The chachalaca is warm brown overall, darker above. It has a small head and bill and a long tail edged in white. The featherless red skin on its throat can be difficult to see.

SOUNDS

A loud, ringing *cha-cha-lac!*, repeated often. Once you hear a chachalaca, you'll never forget it.

HABITAT

Brushy woodlands, parks, and suburban neighborhoods with appropriate habitat.

BACKYARD

Chachalacas will come to feeders for cracked corn, sunflower, and citrus halves. They also visit water features to drink.

Wild Turkey

Meleagris gallopavo   SIZE: 37" (FEMALE) TO 47" (MALE)

The wild turkey is a large dark gamebird commonly found in a variety of wooded and brushy habitats across North America, primarily south of the U.S.–Canada border. Male turkeys (gobblers) fan their tail feathers and puff up their chest in spring courtship display.

FIELD MARKS

A naked red head, a large body covered with iridescent brownish feathers, a long tail, and stout legs set the turkey apart from our other native gamebirds. Older adult males have a "beard" of hairlike feathers hanging from their breast.

SOUNDS

Courting males utter a loud, explosive gobbling call. Calls include *put-put!* and a descending cry (*kyeoo!*) that females give to chicks (poults).

HABITAT

Woods, mixed forests, farm fields, clearings, and wooded swamps. Forages on the ground and roosts in trees at night.

BACKYARD

Flocks of turkeys will visit feeders for cracked corn and sunflower seed, even in suburban neighborhoods. They may scratch out a dust bath in open dry or sandy soil.

Wild Turkeys: males (left) and female (right)

Scaled Quail

Callipepla squamata

SIZE: 10"

Two of this species' nicknames are "blue quail" (for the blue-gray feathers on its chest and back) and "cotton top" (for the white-tipped head feathers). It is fairly common within its range in semiarid desert of the Southwest, where it forms large coveys in fall and winter.

FIELD MARKS
The scaled overall appearance, gray coloration, and crested head are diagnostic. Other quail within its range have more prominent head and face markings. Like other small quail, it runs rather than flies to escape danger.

SOUNDS
Adults call *chee-churr!* as a means of keeping the covey in contact.

HABITAT
Scrubby brushland, barren semidesert, mesas, and ranches.

BACKYARD
Coveys will visit feeding stations for cracked corn and mixed seed scattered on the ground. They also visit water features to drink.

Adult

Gambel's Quail

Callipepla gambelii

SIZE: 11"

California Quail

Callipepla californica

SIZE: 10"

These two similar, medium-sized quail species show a teardrop-shaped topknot on the head. They are nearly always found in small flocks or family groups, feeding on or near the ground. The ranges of these two species have almost no overlap.

FIELD MARKS
Males are more boldly marked than females. They have a black face and throat outlined with white, a black topknot and black bill, a gray chest, and a brownish back. The male Gambel's has a rusty cap and a black spot on a tan, unstreaked belly. The male California has a scaled belly. Females of both species are drab gray-brown overall with a small topknot.

SOUNDS
California: a loud *chi-CAH-go!* Gambel's: one to four loud *cah* notes: *cah-CAH-cah-cah!* or *caaaa!*

HABITAT
California is more coastal in range, Gambel's more in interior desert. Both prefer scrubby habitats, woodland edges, parks, backyards, farms. Gambel's may be more common in human-altered landscapes such as suburbs.

BACKYARD
Both species visit feeding stations for mixed seed and cracked corn, and water features for drinking. They may use open patches of loose dirt for dust bathing.

Gambel's Quail, male

California Quail, male

California Quail, female

GAMBEL'S QUAIL

CALIFORNIA QUAIL

Male (left) and female (right)
Adult male (bottom)

Northern Bobwhite

Colinus virginianus   SIZE: 10"

Once widespread and common, the bobwhite is a chubby, football-shaped, ground-loving bird that has been greatly reduced in number because of habitat loss. Coveys stay together much of the year, foraging and roosting together.

FIELD MARKS
The male's black mask on a white face and throat is conspicuous. He has a dark brown back and pale belly barred with dark markings, and rusty sides. Bobwhites often run to avoid danger, flying only when startled.

SOUNDS
Named for its clearly whistled call: *bob-white!* It also gives a variety of whistles to its flockmates, including calls to signal danger. It is often heard before it is seen.

HABITAT
Brushy farmland, grassland, hedgerows, roadsides, and arid rangeland.

BACKYARD
Bobwhites may visit feeders for mixed seed or cracked corn on the ground in fall and winter if natural food crops are poor. They will use open areas of loose dirt for dust bathing.

Turkey Vulture

Cathartes aura   SIZE: 27"

Across much of North America, the work of cleaning up dead animals such as roadkill falls to this noble bird. Soaring high above the landscape on teetering wings, turkey vultures use their sense of smell and vision to locate carrion.

FIELD MARKS
Dark overall with a featherless red head, turkey vultures show a pale trailing edge to the wings in flight. Long wings and long slender primary feathers help them take advantage of rising air currents. The similar black vulture is smaller overall and shows white primaries in flight.

SOUNDS
Near the nest, gives a low, hollow hiss to scare away predators.

HABITAT
TVs are found in the sky above any habitat type. Roosting sites include towers, dead trees, and billboards. They often nest on fenceposts, where they sometimes warm in the sun with outstretched wings.

BACKYARD
Unless you have a large field where you can offer the carcasses of dead animals, you won't be attracting turkey vultures. However, they probably soar over your property during the summer months.

Adult

Adult in flight

Sharp-shinned Hawk

Accipiter striatus   SIZE: 10"–14"

This is one of our two bird-eating hawks (the other is the Cooper's hawk) that regularly visit backyards for the concentration of birds at feeding stations. Both species may sit and wait for birds to pass by, or they may burst upon a feeder scene in a surprise attack. These predators help keep bird populations healthy.

FIELD MARKS
The "sharpie" is shorter than the Cooper's hawk, with a smaller head, thinner legs, and a square-tipped tail. Adult birds are dark blue-gray on the head and back and are barred with red or orange below. Young birds are streaky brown overall with a brown back. Females are larger than males.

SOUNDS
Call is a shrill *ki-ki-ki,* usually given only near the nest.

HABITAT
Nests in deep forests. Hunts along woodland edges, open woods, parks, and backyards.

BACKYARD
It's illegal to harm birds of prey, so if you'd like to discourage sharp-shinned or Cooper's hawks from making regular meals of the birds at your feeders, stop your feeding operation for a week or two to let the feeder birds disperse.

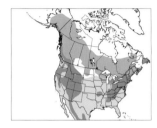

Juvenile female

Adult male

Cooper's Hawk

Accipiter cooperii   SIZE: 14"–20"

This is one of the two common bird-eating hawks frequently seen in backyards—the other is the smaller sharp-shinned hawk. Cooper's hawks are large birds, but they are surprisingly agile fliers when in pursuit of their songbird prey.

FIELD MARKS
A chunky-looking bird. The adult has a blue-gray back and orange breast. The juvenile has a brown back and brown-streaked breast. The female is larger than the male. The Cooper's hawk has a larger head, thicker legs, and broader chest than the sharp-shinned hawk.

SOUNDS
Usually quiet except near the nest, where it may give a loud alarm call: *ka-ka-ka-ka!*

HABITAT
Woodlands and woodland edges. Increasingly common in towns, parks, and backyards, where it hunts for songbirds.

BACKYARD
Accipiters such as the Cooper's and sharp-shinned hawks are surprise hunters. They will sit still along the wood's edge or will soar high in the sky, looking for unsuspecting songbirds to catch. These hawks play an important role in keeping our wild songbird populations healthy—they typically kill sick, injured, or poorly adapted birds.

Immature

Cooper's Hawk, adult

Female

Merlin

Falco columbarius　　　SIZE: 12"

The merlin is a medium-sized falcon, larger than an American kestrel and more heavily streaked overall. Its streakiness makes it look very dark. In flight, the merlin is a direct and speedy flier, and it rarely hovers (as kestrels do) or perches in one place for extended periods.

FIELD MARKS
The male is dark above and the female is brown above, and both are heavily streaked with brown below. Some birds show a dark mustache and hood. The merlin lacks the bold facial marks of the larger peregrine falcon and the rusty coloration of the smaller American kestrel.

SOUNDS
A high-pitched *kii-kii-kii-kii*.

HABITAT
Prefers open country in all seasons, including prairies, beaches, shorelines, and marshes. The merlin is increasingly common in towns and cities, especially in the Great Plains. It is more common in the West, though populations are increasing in the East.

BACKYARD
A merlin may visit your feeders looking for a bird to eat, but this is not a common occurrence (as it is with more regular backyard hunters such as sharp-shinned and Cooper's hawks).

Killdeer

Charadrius vociferous   SIZE: 10½"

Our most common and widespread shorebird can be seen and heard all across the continent in open fields, parks, golf courses, and farms. It nests on open patches of rocky ground, such as the graveled shoulders of roads, and will perform a broken-wing distraction display to lure humans and predators away from its nest.

FIELD MARKS
The white breast is bisected by two black bands (it's the only plover with **two** bands). The face is black, white, and brown. The back and wings are brown. The tail shows a rusty orange base in flight. This species is commonly seen running and stopping on open grassy or muddy habitats.

SOUNDS
This bird is named for its loud call: *killdeee! killdee!* Its alarm call is a rising, nervous *dee-dee-dee-dee!* It calls at night and anytime danger is near.

HABITAT
Farm fields, playing fields, airports, mudflats, and shorelines.

BACKYARD
If you have a large open, grassy yard or a wide gravel driveway, killdeer may forage or even nest on your property.

Adult

Rock Pigeon

Columba livia SIZE: 12½"

Also known as the rock dove, and feral or domestic pigeon, this species was introduced from Europe and now thrives all across North America. It is often seen perched on building ledges, bridges, farm silos, and old barns.

FIELD MARKS
Plumage varies, but the most common form is gray with a white rump and a black tail tip. Other plumage variations include birds that are white, warm brown, and mottled. The body is plump, the head small.

SOUNDS
Call is a soft, low-toned *coo-caroo-coo*. When a rock pigeon is startled into flight, its wings clap together audibly.

HABITAT
Found primarily in urban settings such as building ledges and bridges but also in rural areas near old barns and silos, where it prefers to roost and nest.

BACKYARD
Rock pigeons can dominate a bird feeder with their large size and equally large appetites. They eat cracked corn and mixed seed as well as sunflower bits. To discourage them, offer food only in small tube feeders. Do not offer food on the ground, on low platform feeders, or in large hopper feeders.

Adult, gray form

Band-tailed Pigeon

Patagioenas fasciata SIZE: 15"

A chunky pigeon of the mountain West, similar to the rock pigeon. Unlike the urban-dwelling rock pigeon, this bird prefers woodland habitat and often is found perched in trees.

FIELD MARKS

A large all-dark bird with a pale tan tip on its gray tail. A white band across the nape of the neck and a yellow bill tipped in black set this pigeon apart from its relatives. In perfect light, a patch of green iridescent feathers can be seen on the hind neck.

SOUNDS

A series of hollow-sounding notes, *whoo-whoo-whooooo*, which are often mistaken for a daylight-calling owl.

HABITAT

Mountain forests and wooded canyons, especially those with many oaks. Suburban parks and thickly wooded neighborhoods may also host this species.

BACKYARD

Visits backyards for roosting or nesting in tall trees. May visit feeders in well-wooded backyards.

Adult

Eurasian Collared-Dove

Streptopelia decaocto   SIZE: 13"

A recent immigrant to North America from the Caribbean, this large pale dove is spreading rapidly across the continent. It has a stockier body than the similar-sized mourning dove. It loves to perch on power lines.

FIELD MARKS
Paler than a mourning dove, the Eurasian collared-dove shows an obvious black collar. Its tail is fanned, not tapered like the mourning dove's.

SOUNDS
Its loud cooing call is a common sound where this species is already established: *coo-COO-cuh*.

HABITAT
Cities, towns, suburban neighborhoods, and power lines along roadways.

BACKYARD
This dove will come to bird feeders for almost any kind of seed or grain. In some areas, it is so numerous it's becoming a feeder pest.

Adult

White-winged Dove

Zenaida asiatica   SIZE: 11¾"

The white-winged dove is a desert and arid-habitat bird, similar to the more widespread mourning dove but with two large white wing patches. It is common year-round from southern Florida west to southernmost California.

FIELD MARKS

This dove is gray-brown overall with large white wing patches and a shorter, rounded (not tapered) tail tipped in white.

SOUNDS

Song is a hoarse-sounding *who cooks for you?*

HABITAT

Dry brushy areas, mesquite groves, riparian woods, towns, parks, and backyards.

BACKYARD

Visits feeders for mixed seed scattered on the ground or on low platform feeders. Also visits water features.

Adult

Mourning Dove

Zenaida
macroura

SIZE: 12"

Our most common native dove species, the mourning dove is named for its mournful cooing call, which it may give in any month of the year.

FIELD MARKS
This is a slender brown dove, smaller than a rock pigeon, with a long tapered tail edged in white. It has a small-headed appearance. Its neck may take on some pink and green iridescence in direct sunlight.

SOUNDS
The mourning dove utters a sad-sounding call: *coo-ahh-coocoocoo*. When startled, it explodes into flight, causing its wings to whistle.

HABITAT
Cornfields, farms, parks, open woodlands, and urban and suburban backyards.

BACKYARD
This dove is common at bird feeders, where it eats sunflower hearts, cracked corn, and mixed seed on the ground or on low platform feeders. It drinks from water sources using its bill as a straw.

Inca Dove

Columbina inca   SIZE: 8¼"–8½"

Appearing scalloped overall, this small gray-tan dove may go unnoticed until it bursts into flight.

FIELD MARKS
The Inca dove is larger than the common ground-dove and has a longer tail prominently edged in white. Both species show rufous in the wings in flight, but the Inca dove has a black bill (the common ground-dove has an orange bill tipped in black).

SOUNDS
Song is two repetitive notes: *cooo-coo.*

HABITAT
Scrub and mesquite habitats, usually near human habitation, including parks, farms, and backyards.

BACKYARD
Inca doves visit feeders for mixed seed scattered on the ground or on a low platform feeder. They will also visit water features to drink.

Adult

Common Ground-Dove

Columbina passerina   SIZE: 6½"

This small dove looks like a miniature mourning dove until it bursts into flight, showing bright rufous outer wings. It resembles the Inca dove, which is much more scaly overall and has a longer tail.

FIELD MARKS
Pale gray overall, with a black-tipped orange bill and pale head and breast. The head and breast are scaled with black. In flight, it shows rufous in the outer wing and a stubby black tail with white outer tips.

SOUNDS
A two-syllabled *woo-hoo* rising in tone, repeated in a series.

HABITAT
A common resident of open grassy areas, roadsides, brushland, farms, and parks.

BACKYARD
Forages on the ground below feeders for mixed seed and cracked corn. Often found in small flocks.

Adult

Greater Roadrunner

Geococcyx californianus   SIZE: 22"–23"

Looking nothing like its cartoon namesake, the greater roadrunner is the largest North American cuckoo. Roadrunners spend most of their lives on the ground hunting lizards, snakes, small mammals, and birds.

FIELD MARKS

The roadrunner is a large, long-tailed bird, streaky brown and white overall, with a dark crest that it can raise and lower. It has a powerful bill and stout legs with long toes. A patch of featherless skin behind the eye is blue and red.

SOUNDS

Song sounds like a dove's: *coo-coo-coo-coo-coo-coo*, dropping in pitch.

HABITAT

Roadrunners are year-round residents in open country, desert scrub, mesquite groves, parks, and backyards.

BACKYARD

Roadrunners will visit backyards for odd food items, including meat scraps and dog food. They will capture and eat small birds at feeders, including hummingbirds.

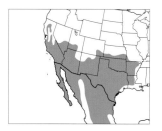

Adult

Gray morph

Eastern Screech-Owl

Megascops asio   SIZE: 8½"

This common small owl of the East is rarely noticed because of its nocturnal habits, quiet ways, and cryptic coloration. Both red and gray forms exist, but gray is more often encountered.

FIELD MARKS
With plumage the color and pattern of tree bark, screech-owls are difficult to see on their daytime roosts. They can raise and lower their ear tufts to help them blend in. Listen for screech-owls calling on summer evenings. On sunny winter days, check tree cavities for owls peeking out to absorb some of the sun's warmth.

SOUNDS
Call is a soft, quavering whinny that descends several times and ends in a tremolo on a single, lower note.

HABITAT
Woodlands with older trees that have natural cavities. Also common in parks and wooded neighborhoods in cities and towns.

BACKYARD
Screech-owls will use nest boxes placed high on trunks of large trees. They may visit water features late at night to drink and bathe. They do not visit feeders, except at night to catch mice attracted to fallen seed.

Chimney Swift

Chaetura pelagica SIZE: 5¼"

The most common description of the chimney swift is that it looks like a cigar with wings. It is nearly always seen on the wing. Named for its habit of nesting in human-built chimneys, it formerly nested in hollow trees, caves, and on rocky cliff faces. This is the only swift in the East.

FIELD MARKS
Chimney swifts are dusky gray overall with long slender wings. Their flight style is several rapid wing flaps followed by a short glide. In late summer, pre-migratory roosts form in large chimneys or silos, and clouds of chimney swifts can be observed swirling to the roost at dusk.

SOUNDS
A loud, twittering chatter. Swifts call frequently in flight, especially when others of their kind are present.

HABITAT
Open skies over cities, towns, and suburban neighborhoods. Chimney swifts need open-topped chimneys for nesting and roosting.

BACKYARD
Chimney swifts will forage over an eastern backyard at some point in the warm months. They will use specially designed nesting towers erected in open habitat. They do not visit feeders or water features.

Adult male

Ruby-throated Hummingbird

Archilochus colubris   SIZE: 3¾"

The ruby-throat is the only common hummingbird of the East in spring and summer. Most ruby-throats leave for the Neotropics in winter, though a few overwinter in the Gulf states. In fall and winter, any hummingbird visiting a feeder should be carefully checked—it may be a vagrant species from the West.

FIELD MARKS
Adult males have a magenta throat patch, or gorget, which can appear black in bright sunlight. The chest is pale; the belly greenish; and the crown, back, and tail iridescent green. Females and young birds are green above, white below.

SOUNDS
Calls are high squeaky or sputtering notes. The male's wings hum in courtship display, which is a long looping pendulum-shaped flight performed for a perched female.

HABITAT
Usually seen at or near flowering plants, vines, and trees in gardens, woodland edges, and backyards.

BACKYARD
Ruby-throats readily come to gardens or planters with nectar-producing flowers. They also visit feeders for sugar water.

Adult female

Black-chinned Hummingbird

Archilochus alexandri   SIZE: 3¾"

This is the most widespread hummingbird in the West. The male's gorget flashes deep purple in the right light; in poor light it can appear black. Other male hummingbirds may also appear to have black gorgets in poor light.

FIELD MARKS
Both sexes are bright green on the head, back, and tail. Males show a clean white bib below the dark purple gorget. Females look similar to female ruby-throated hummingbirds.

SOUNDS
The wings make a humming sound in flight. Chasing birds give a series of twitters and buzzes. Call is a soft *chew!*

HABITAT
Common in wooded foothills and canyons and along the ocean coast.

BACKYARD
Visits backyards and gardens for nectar-producing flowers and for nectar at hummingbird feeders.

Adult male

Anna's Hummingbird

Calypte anna   SIZE: 4"

The male Anna's is our only hummingbird with a bright red crown, which combined with his ruby red gorget and emerald green back, makes for an impressive bird. This species is common along the Pacific Coast all year long. In spring and summer, the male performs a remarkable courtship flight: soaring in a pendulum-shaped loop in view of a perched female, he makes a loud popping sound at the bottom of each loop.

FIELD MARKS

The male's crown and gorget are brilliant ruby in good light but can appear black in bright sunshine. A greenish back and smudgy green belly make the Anna's appear "messier" than other hummers. Females may have some red spots on the otherwise white throat. At 4 inches in length, the Anna's is larger than most other widespread western hummingbirds.

SOUNDS

A series of raspy notes and chattery buzzes is what passes for the Anna's song, which the male usually delivers while perched.

HABITAT

Common in brushy habitat in the westernmost states from Canada to Mexico. Any habitat with nectar-producing flowers, including parks, gardens, and backyards, can host this species.

BACKYARD

Hummingbird feeders and nectar-producing flowers will attract the Anna's hummingbird throughout its somewhat narrow range.

Adult male

Costa's Hummingbird

Calypte costae   SIZE: 3½"

Male Costa's hummingbirds have a striking, deep purple crown and a gorget that extends downward like a Fu Manchu mustache. This small hummingbird has a diagnostic call—see below.

FIELD MARKS
The male's gorget shape and color are unique among our hummingbirds. The female is green above and white below. This species is similar to the black-chinned hummingbird, which is slightly larger. The male black-chinned lacks the extended gorget and purple crown of the male Costa's.

SOUNDS
Call is a high-pitched, tinny *tink-tink-tink-tink*. Male's display call is a rising *ziiiing!*

HABITAT
Desert scrub, chaparral, dry washes with flowering plants, backyards, and gardens.

BACKYARD
Visits gardens for flowering plants and feeders for nectar.

Adult male

Calliope Hummingbird

Stellula calliope   SIZE: 3¼"

This is the smallest bird in North America north of Mexico. A common visitor to feeders and gardens within its range, the Calliope sometimes holds its tail cocked upward while hovering to feed.

FIELD MARKS
The male's gorget of magenta feathers may be flared open or held together, forming an inverted V on the throat. The male is green above, white below. The female is green above and white-bellied with buffy flanks. Calliopes look very short-tailed and small compared with other hummingbirds.

SOUNDS
Various chips and twitters in flight. The male gives a high-pitched *tsee-see* in courtship flight.

HABITAT
Mountain meadows and open canyons. Often found near water. Present in summer only.

BACKYARD
Readily visits feeders and gardens with blooming, nectar-producing plants.

Broad-tailed Hummingbird

Selasphorus platycercus   SIZE: 4"

This hummingbird is often heard before it is seen, because the wings of the adult male produce a loud, whistled trill as he flies. The species is common throughout the inland mountain West.

FIELD MARKS
Males and females are metallic green above with a white breast and belly. Males have a magenta gorget. Females have a speckled throat and buffy sides. Both sexes look similar to the ruby-throated hummingbird of the East.

SOUNDS
In addition to the wing trill of the male in flight, broad-taileds produce a high-pitched chattering song, usually from a perch. Call is a loud *chit!*

HABITAT
Mountain forests and wooded canyons.

BACKYARD
A common visitor at hummingbird feeders and in gardens and parks with flowering plants.

Adult male

Rufous Hummingbird

Selasphorus rufus   SIZE: 3¾"

Rusty, red, and white overall, this is our only North American hummingbird with an all-rufous back. Only males can be separated visually from the very similar Allen's hummingbird. Female rufous and Allen's hummingbirds are indistinguishable.

FIELD MARKS
The male has a rufous back and tail, a bright red gorget, and a white chest. The similar Allen's hummingbird male has a green back. The rufous hummingbird aggressively defends food sources.

SOUNDS
Makes a variety of vocal chips and twitters. The male's wings whistle in flight, especially during courtship display.

HABITAT
Forests, woodland edges, mountain meadows, gardens, backyards, and parks.

BACKYARD
Visits flower gardens and feeders for nectar. This species is increasingly regular as a fall and winter vagrant to feeders and gardens in the East and Southeast.

Adult male

Allen's Hummingbird

Selasphorus sasin SIZE: 3¾"

This rufous, green, and white hummingbird is found along the Pacific Coast. It is very similar to the more widespread rufous hummingbird. Females of the two species are indistinguishable (except to the birds themselves).

FIELD MARKS
Males have a bright orange gorget, white belly, green crown and back, and rufous tail. (Rufous hummingbird males have a mostly rufous back and tail.)

SOUNDS
In flight, the male's wings make a loud whirr. Call is a loud, piercing *kvikk!* The male often gives it during swooping, pendulum courtship display flight.

HABITAT
Woodlands, wooded parks, brushy gardens, backyards.

BACKYARD
Visits backyards for nectar at feeders and for nectar-producing flowers.

Adult male

Lewis's Woodpecker

Melanerpes lewis   SIZE: 10¾"–11"

Lewis's is a large dark woodpecker of open forest habitat of the West. This species was discovered on the Lewis and Clark Expedition and named for Meriwether Lewis. In flight, the Lewis's woodpecker appears crowlike, lacking the undulating flight pattern of most other woodpeckers.

FIELD MARKS
The dark green head and back can appear black in poor light. The gray neck and breast, red face, and pink belly are diagnostic field marks. Less active than other woodpeckers, Lewis's will sit quietly on a perch for long periods, sometimes sallying forth to catch flying insects.

SOUNDS
Usually silent. May utter a harsh *churr* as a contact call.

HABITAT
Prefers open oak or ponderosa pine woodlands but is also found in riparian woods, orchards, and wooded farmlots.

BACKYARD
If you live within this species' range, the best attractant is an oak tree with lots of acorns. This species will use dead limbs and snags as flycatching perches and will visit feeders for suet, suet dough, peanuts, and nuts. It may use nest boxes appropriate for flickers.

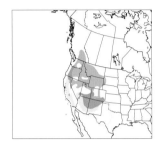

Adult

Red-headed Woodpecker

Melanerpes
erythrocephalus

SIZE: 9¼"

The bold red, black, and white colors of the red-headed woodpecker make this bird easy to identify even at great distances, especially in flight when it flashes black and white. Populations are declining throughout its range because of habitat loss and competition for nesting cavities from other birds.

FIELD MARKS

Adults show a full hood of deep red, a pale gray bill, a black back, and black wings and tail intersected with large patches of white. The breast and belly are white. Juveniles have a streaky gray-brown head, breast, and back.

SOUNDS

Call is a loud, excited-sounding *quee-ahh!* It is higher pitched and more nasal than that of the red-bellied woodpecker.

HABITAT

Open woods, woodlots in farm country, parks with large trees. Prefers nut-bearing trees such as oaks, beeches, and hickories. Nests semi-colonially in woodlots with standing dead trees.

BACKYARD

May visit feeders located close to nesting colonies, or on migration. Prefers cracked corn, suet, suet dough, mealworms, peanuts, sunflower seed, and fruit. Rarely uses nest boxes but will excavate nest cavities in standing dead trees, which is reason enough to not remove all dead trees from your property.

Adult

Acorn Woodpecker

Melanerpes formicivorus   SIZE: 9"

This is a medium-sized woodpecker of the West. Acorn woodpeckers form large colonies that are nonmigratory. They are famous for creating large caches of acorns stored in individual holes drilled in dead trees and house siding.

FIELD MARKS
The acorn woodpecker is black above and white below. The bold clown makeup on its face is distinctive. The white eye with a dark iris stands out on the black face. The sexes are very similar; the female has a black patch on her forehead.

SOUNDS
A noisy, harsh *shack-up, shack-up!*

HABITAT
Oak woods of the West. This bird relies on acorns as an important food source. It also flycatches (eats insects caught in flight).

BACKYARD
Visits backyards for acorns in oak trees, peanuts, suet, and water at birdbaths.

Golden-fronted Woodpecker

Melanerpes aurifrons   SIZE: 9½"

This medium-sized woodpecker replaces the closely related red-bellied woodpecker in central and western Texas and southwestern Oklahoma. Its name comes from the patch of gold feathers on the forehead, which is most noticeable on adult males.

FIELD MARKS
The male has two yellow patches and a red crown on his gray head. The nape patch may appear orange on some birds. The female has duller yellow patches and no red. The back is zebra striped, the tail is black, and the rump flashes white in flight.

SOUNDS
Calls include a loud, piercing *churrr* and a series of flicker-like notes: *kek-kek-kek-kek-kek*.

HABITAT
Mesquite thickets, dry woodlands and groves, backyards, and parks.

BACKYARD
Readily visits feeders for seed and for citrus fruit halves. Also visits water features.

Adult male

Red-bellied Woodpecker

Melanerpes carolinus   SIZE: 9¼"

Common in the eastern and southeastern United States, this woodpecker is slowly spreading north, thanks in part to food at bird feeders. It is sometimes confused with the red-headed woodpecker, which has a full hood of red.

FIELD MARKS
The red-bellied is a medium-sized woodpecker with a full "Mohawk" of red in the male (females show a tan forehead) and a zebra-striped back. The red belly for which the species is named is difficult to see on birds clinging to tree trunks or branches.

SOUNDS
Call is a loud, burry *churrrr!* Red-bellies drum loudly on hollow trees or metal house chimneys in territorial and mating displays.

HABITAT
Can be found in almost any forested habitat, including wooded backyards and parks.

BACKYARD
Readily visits feeders for sunflower seeds, peanuts, suet, and suet dough, and will even drink nectar from hummingbird feeders. May use nest boxes placed in large trees and filled with wood chips.

Adult male

Yellow-bellied Sapsucker

Sphyrapicus varius   SIZE: 8½"

Red-naped Sapsucker

Sphyrapicus nuchalis   SIZE: 8½"

Our two common and widespread sapsucker species are similar in many ways: appearance, habits, voice, and willingness to visit backyard feeding stations. Red-naped sapsuckers are found throughout the West in spring and summer, migrating southward in winter. Yellow-bellied sapsuckers nest across northern North America and move to the Southeast in winter.

FIELD MARKS
These species can best be identified by range. Males of both species have a red crown and throat; red-naped has a red patch on the back of the head. The bold white wing patches of both species help separate them from other woodpeckers.

SOUNDS
Both species give a nasal mewing call: *myear.* The territorial drumming pattern is also distinctive: *taptaptaptap- tap——tap—tap.*

HABITAT
Coniferous and mixed woodlands, orchards, aspens, and birches. Sapsuckers drill small holes in rows on tree trunks and return later to drink the sap that oozes from the holes.

BACKYARD
Look for lines of small drilled holes—evidence that sapsuckers have visited your backyard trees. They will also visit feeders for fruit, suet, suet dough, peanuts, peanut butter, and sunflower hearts, and nectar at hummingbird feeders.

YELLOW-BELLIED SAPSUCKER

RED-NAPED SAPSUCKER

Yellow-bellied Sapsucker: adult male

Red-naped Sapsucker: adult male

Ladder-backed Woodpecker

Picoides scalaris   SIZE: 7¼"

This woodpecker of the desert Southwest is named for the horizontal black-and-white stripes on its back.

FIELD MARKS
Black-and-white back, black spots on a tan breast, and a black and tan face are this species' key field marks. The male has a bright red crown and nape. The female has a black crown and nape. This species is very similar to the Nuttall's woodpecker

of California. It is easiest to separate the two by checking their range maps.

SOUNDS
A series of loud, rattling notes: *chee-kee-kee-kee-keee!* fading in volume. Call is similar to that of the downy woodpecker: *pick!*

HABITAT
Dry brushland, mesquite thickets, riparian woods, and wooded canyons.

BACKYARD
This woodpecker visits feeders for suet, suet dough, peanuts, fruit, and sunflower hearts.

Downy Woodpecker

Picoides pubescens   SIZE: 6½"–6¾"

Hairy Woodpecker

Picoides villosus   SIZE: 9"–9¼"

Remembering this phrase can help you separate these two look-alike woodpeckers: "Downy is dinky, hairy is huge." This refers both to the birds' respective body sizes and the relative length of their bills.

FIELD MARKS
Both species are mainly black on the back and white below. Hairy woodpeckers show an obvious white patch in the middle of the black back and unmarked white outer tail feathers. The hairy's bill is longer than its head is wide.

The downy's bill is shorter than its head is wide, and its outer tail feathers are marked with black. Males of both species have a red patch at the back of the head.

SOUNDS
Downy: a rapid whinny dropping in pitch. Call is a flat *pik!* Hairy: loud rattle call does not descend in pitch. Call is a sharp, loud *peek!*

Both species drum their bills on hollow logs and downspouts to announce their territorial claims.

HABITAT
Both species prefer forests, parks with large trees, and backyards. Hairy woodpeckers prefer older, larger trees than downies do.

BACKYARD
Both species commonly visit feeders for sunflower seed, suet, suet dough, peanuts, and fruit bits.

Downy Woodpecker: adult female

Hairy Woodpecker: adult male

DOWNY WOODPECKER

HAIRY WOODPECKER

Northern Flicker

Colaptes auratus   SIZE: 12½"

A woodpecker that does much of its foraging on the ground, the northern flicker comes in two color variations: yellow-shafted and red-shafted. The smaller gilded flicker is a separate species with a limited range in the desert Southwest.

FIELD MARKS
The northern flicker has many field marks: an obvious white rump and brown back, a buff breast with black spots, and a black half-collar. The male has a mustache (red in red-shafted and black in yellow-shafted). The female does not have facial markings.

SOUNDS
Flickers give a variety of calls: a loud, ringing *week-week-week-week-week*. Also *klee-ear!* And *flicker-flicker-flicker*, for which the birds are named.

HABITAT
Open woodlands, forests, parks, and towns with large trees. Flickers often forage on the ground for ants, using their tongue to extract them from anthills.

BACKYARD
Flickers may visit feeders for suet, suet dough, peanuts, and fruit, but they are more likely to forage on open lawns and open ground for ants.

Adult male

Pileated Woodpecker

Dryocopus pileatus

SIZE: 17"

The largest of our common woodpeckers, the pileated is a woodland generalist—able to eat a variety of foods. It has adjusted well to changing habitats. The even larger ivory-billed woodpecker, now thought to be extinct, relied on very special old-growth habitat. When the habitat disappeared, so did the ivory-billed woodpecker.

FIELD MARKS
A mostly black bird, as large as a crow, with a bright red crest. Males also have a red mustache. Females lack the mustache and have a black forehead. In flight, the wings of both sexes flash black and white.

SOUNDS
A loud, ringing call, *yii-yii-yii-yii-yii*, which is louder and slower than the northern flicker's call. Pileateds often call in flight or just before flying. Mates call to each other frequently. They also drum loudly on hollow logs and trees.

HABITAT
A year-round resident of wooded groves, parks, suburban neighborhoods, and mixed forests with large trees.

BACKYARD
Lucky bird watchers attract this bird with large suet feeders, suet dough, peanuts, and peanut butter. Pileateds will also forage for ants and grubs on old tree stumps and decaying or downed trees.

Adult female

Eastern Phoebe

Sayornis phoebe   SIZE: 7"

This medium-sized, drab flycatcher has adapted easily to live near human habitation, often nesting in barns, on porches, and under eaves. An early migrant, the phoebe is considered by many to be a reliable harbinger of spring.

FIELD MARKS
Drab gray-green above and pale below, with a dark-headed appearance. Sexes are alike. This species can be identified at a distance by its habit of constantly flicking its tail up and down. It flies out from an exposed perch to catch insects in flight, often returning to the original perch.

SOUNDS
Regularly calls out its name: *fee-bee* or *fee-bree!* Also gives a soft, sweet-sounding chip note: *tchup!*

HABITAT
Wooded habitat near water. A cavity nester with a preference for building its mud-and-grass nest in old barns, sheds, and under bridges.

BACKYARD
Phoebes may nest in your backyard if there is a safe and handy ledge, an old barn, or an outbuilding. They typically do not visit feeders but may visit a water feature.

Say's Phoebe

Sayornis saya SIZE: 7½"

Common in open country, this medium-sized dark flycatcher constantly pumps its dark tail. It spends its summers in the West, from Alaska to Mexico, migrating in fall as far south as the Neotropics. Some winter in the desert Southwest.

FIELD MARKS
Say's phoebe is dark overall with a warm buff belly and a black tail. It is darker overall than other western flycatchers, except for the black phoebe. The sexes are similar.

SOUNDS
Calls frequently and in flight: *pit-pweer!*

HABITAT
Open country, scrublands, parks, ranch yards, and canyons. Often found near old abandoned buildings, and may nest there.

BACKYARD
This is not a regular backyard visitor, but it is frequently found near human settlements in otherwise open, treeless country.

Loggerhead Shrike

Lanius ludovicianus   SIZE: 9"

The smaller of our two shrike species, the loggerhead shrike looks superficially like a northern mockingbird. But the shrike's powerful, flesh-tearing black bill, larger head, and blacker wings and tail help tell it from the mockingbird. Shrikes catch insects, birds, rodents, and snakes and impale them on barbed wire or plant thorns to aid in tearing the prey into small edible pieces.

FIELD MARKS
The shrike is gray and black above and pale gray below, with an obvious black mask and bill. Its wings flash white in flight, like those of a mockingbird (which has gray, not black wings).

SOUNDS
Song is a surprisingly melodic series of warbles at low volume, with harsh notes interspersed. Call is *shack-shack!*

HABITAT
Scrubby brushland and open country with barbed-wire fences or thorny bushes. Often perches on wires, fenceposts, and treetops while scanning for prey.

BACKYARD
May visit feeding stations looking for birds to eat.

Gray Jay

Perisoreus canadensis

SIZE: 11½"

Known as the "camp robber" for its bold food-grabbing ways, the gray jay is a chunky bird with a stout bill and crestless head. It inhabits the woods of the far North and higher elevations in western mountains.

FIELD MARKS
This jay is dark gray above and pale gray below, with a dark hood across the back of the head. It has a pale forehead and a large dark eye. The bill appears short for a jay.

SOUNDS
Call is a soft, two-noted *wee-ohh!* Also utters other short raspy notes.

HABITAT
Northern boreal forests of fir and spruce. Common near campgrounds, parks, trails.

BACKYARD
Will visit backyards for suet and meat scraps. Tame gray jays are common at woodland resorts, ski lodges, and campgrounds.

Steller's Jay

Cyanocitta
stelleri

SIZE: 11½"

The Steller's jay is the larger of our two crested jays, beating out the blue jay by about half an inch in length. Its large size, bold habits, and loud voice make it a commonly encountered bird.

FIELD MARKS
This jay is very dark overall, with a black head, neck and back and deep blue wings and tail. No other western jay is as dark or has a crested head. The sexes are similar.

SOUNDS
Utters a variety of harsh, loud notes, typically *shack-shack-shack-shack!*

HABITAT
Coniferous and pine-oak woods, parks, campsites, and backyards.

BACKYARD
Visits feeding stations for almost any food but especially for peanuts and food scraps. Also visits water features to drink and bathe. Often begs for handouts at campsites and resort lodges.

Blue Jay

Cyanocitta cristata   SIZE: 11"

This large, bold, and noisy bird is often found in loose flocks. Like other members of the corvid family (crows, jays, etc.), it has a reputation for intelligence and adaptability, eating a wide variety of foods and storing surplus food for later consumption.

FIELD MARKS

This is the only large, crested, blue-colored bird in the East. The crest and back are blue, the face and belly white. Blue jays flash white wing bars and outer tail feathers in flight. They are similar to the Steller's jays of the West, which are slightly larger and darker overall, lacking any white in the wings or tail.

SOUNDS

A harsh, scolding *jaay!* Also gives a variety of unusual calls, including bell-like whistles, rusty squeaks, and toots. Will imitate the calls of hawks.

HABITAT

Any wooded habitat (especially those with nut-bearing trees), backyards, parks.

BACKYARD

Blue jays eat almost anything at bird feeders, including peanuts, suet, suet dough, sunflower seeds, fruit, and cracked corn. They also visit birdbaths. They will scream like a hawk to scare other birds away from feeders.

Western Scrub-Jay

Aphelocoma californica   SIZE: 11¼"

The western scrub-jay is a widely distributed member of the corvid family found in a wide range of habitats throughout the West. Two species with limited ranges have been split off from the western scrub-jay: the Florida scrub-jay of central Florida and the island scrub-jay of California's Santa Cruz Island.

FIELD MARKS
This jay is a noisy and obvious bird with a dark blue head, white throat, gray back, and long dark blue tail. It is the same size as the Steller's jay but lacks that species' crested head.

SOUNDS
Call is a harsh, rasping *kresh-kresh-kresh!*

HABITAT
Woodlands, particularly those containing oaks (acorns are a main food source), riparian areas, parks, and residential areas.

BACKYARD
An eager feeder visitor. Eats almost anything, including peanuts, suet, suet dough, fruit, nuts, and sunflower seed. Also visits water features to drink and bathe.

Black-billed Magpie

Pica hudsonia SIZE: 18½"

It's hard to mistake the black-billed magpie for anything else, with its bold markings and impressive large size. In flight the magpie flashes black and white. Where you find one magpie, you usually find a flock.

FIELD MARKS
The magpie's long black tail gives it a crow-sized appearance. Its bold black head, wings, and body, which is bisected with white, can appear greenish blue in direct sunlight. A close relative, the yellow-billed magpie, is found only in the central valleys of California, and features, not surprisingly, a yellow bill.

SOUNDS
Common call is a harsh, croaky *quah-quah-quah-quah.*

HABITAT
Open brushy country, agricultural fields, forest edges, rangeland with scattered clumps of conifers.

BACKYARD
The magpie will scavenge for food in backyards, even boldly stealing food from picnic tables and deck railings. It eats peanuts, pieces of bread, bits of fruit, suet, and meat and other food scraps.

American Crow

Corvus brachyrhynchos   SIZE: 17½"

This is a large all-black bird with a dark eye and stout bill. Crows are often found in noisy flocks during fall and winter and in smaller family groups in spring and summer. They have adapted well to human habitats despite being persecuted as agricultural pests.

FIELD MARKS
The American crow is all black with a fan-shaped tail. Two similar species are the common raven and the fish crow. The raven is larger overall with a bigger head, larger bill, and spade-shaped tail. The fish crow is smaller and has a distinctively nasal, two-part call: *ah-ahh!*

SOUNDS
Nearly everyone knows the *caw-caw-caw* of the crow. But crows also give a variety of other calls, including rattles, gurgles, and nasal scolds.

HABITAT
Common across much of North America in a variety of habitats from backyards and city parks to farm fields and woodlands.

BACKYARD
Visits backyards for any food it can get, including cracked corn or suet at feeders, food scraps on compost piles, and even food from pet dishes.

Purple Martin

Progne subis SIZE: 8"

The purple martin is our largest swallow. In flight, the all-dark male looks similar to a European starling. Martins in the East are totally reliant on human-supplied housing. Martins in the West still often use natural cavities or old woodpecker holes.

FIELD MARKS
The adult male is dark blue-purple overall with long wings and a deeply notched tail. Adult females and young birds are blue-backed and dirty gray below. The flight style of this species is several fast flaps followed by a long graceful glide.

SOUNDS
Song is a burbling series of throaty notes, clicks, and twitters. Call is a descending *tyew, tyew.*

HABITAT
Martins prefer to live in open country near human habitation and/or near water, such as on farms, parks, golf courses, and lakefronts. They capture flying insects on the wing.

BACKYARD
Large open yards and fields can host nesting purple martins in "condo"-like nest boxes. Some colonies may contain hundreds of pairs. Martins will pick up eggshell bits scattered on a roof, driveway, or platform feeder.

Adult male

Adult male

Tree Swallow

Tachycineta bicolor   SIZE: 5¾"

Tree swallows are common all across North America in summer, in wooded habitats near water and in open meadows where there are human-supplied nesting cavities. In recent years, this species has expanded its breeding range to the south. In fall, thousands of tree swallows form pre-migration flocks, roosting in marsh vegetation and on wires and fences.

FIELD MARKS
Tree swallows are metallic blue-green on the head, wings, back, and tail and white below. Males are darker green than females. The similar violet-green swallow of the West has a white face and white areas on its rump.

SOUNDS
Calls, often given in flight, are one or two syllables: *cheet* or *chi-vleet!* Also gives a liquid, burbling twitter.

HABITAT
The tree swallow is named for its habit of nesting in holes in trees. It cannot excavate its own nest hole, so it uses old woodpecker holes and natural cavities. It usually forages near water or over open meadows.

BACKYARD
If you have a large open grassy area or a wooded pond on your property, you may be able to attract tree swallows with nest boxes. Tree and barn swallows will take eggshell bits from a sidewalk or deck railing. Tree swallows will also take white feathers if you offer them when they are nest building.

Violet-green Swallow

Tachycineta thalassin   SIZE: 5¼"

Throughout the West, from Alaska to Mexico, the summer skies are home to the violet-green swallow. Like its relative the tree swallow, this species nests in cavities such as old woodpecker holes, as well as in loose colonies on rocky cliff faces and canyons. Violet-green swallows return later in spring than many migrants.

FIELD MARKS
The white on the face and white patches on the rump help separate the violet-green swallow from the larger and more widespread tree swallow (which has a dark face and rump).

SOUNDS
Calls include a rapid series of chips and two-part notes: *chew-it, chew-it, chi-chi-chi.*

HABITAT
Open woodlands, foothills, canyons, and suburban neighborhoods. Forages in any habitat. Nests in loose colonies in canyons, on cliff faces, and in tree cavities.

BACKYARD
Two ways to attract violet-green swallows to your backyard are by placing nest boxes and by offering crushed eggshells. Nesting females will eat the eggshell bits to replenish the calcium they lose during egg production.

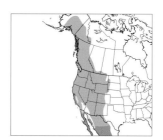

Cliff Swallow

Petrochelidon pyrrhonota　　SIZE: 5½"

This species is very similar to the barn swallow but lacks the deeply forked swallow tail. Where you see one cliff swallow, you usually see many, since this species nests in large colonies. Cliff swallows build thin jug-shaped nests out of wet mud—one billful at a time—and adhere them to a cliff face, bridge support, or barn siding.

FIELD MARKS
A pale tan forehead, or "headlight," and a "taillight" on the rump set this species apart from the barn swallow and make it easy to pick out among flying flocks of swallows.

SOUNDS
Call is a series of squeaky notes that sound like a toy robot. Flying birds call often, and nesting colonies are very noisy.

HABITAT
A summer resident across much of the continent, cliff swallows are most common where there are viable nest sites nearby. They forage over water, farm fields, and meadows.

BACKYARD
Not a regular backyard visitor in habitats lacking nesting opportunities (such as old barns, open caves, culverts, or bridges).

Barn Swallow

Hirundo rustica   SIZE: 6¾"

Perhaps our most graceful flier, the barn swallow swoops and sails across fields, gardens, and backyards throughout North America. Its deeply forked tail and long wings allow the barn swallow to fly swiftly and expertly enough to capture flying insects.

FIELD MARKS

A rusty face and throat and orange belly are offset by a deep blue back and tail. The deeply forked tail is unique among our swallows. The similar-looking cliff swallow has a slightly notched tail and a pale rump.

SOUNDS

Barn swallows call and chatter almost constantly and are far more vocal than our other swallows. Primary call is a series of squeaky notes: *pit-pitpit-pit-pitpit-pitpit*. A scold note (a harsh, coarse *kvit-kvit-kvit*) is given in response to danger, especially near the nest.

HABITAT

Barn swallows forage low over meadows, gardens, ponds, and other open areas, but they are most common near their nest sites, which include old barns (hence their name), abandoned buildings, bridges, and culverts.

BACKYARD

Barn swallows will adhere their mud-and-grass nests to the sides of any rough surface, such as inside a garden shed or old barn. In spring and summer, they are attracted to eggshell bits left on a driveway, sidewalk, deck railing, or roof.

Carolina Chickadee

Poecile carolinensis   SIZE: 4¾"

Black-capped Chickadee

Poecile atricapillus   SIZE: 5¼"

These two small charming woodland sprites are nearly identical in appearance. Inquisitive by nature, they are often the first birds to visit a new feeder in the backyard.

FIELD MARKS
A dark cap and throat are offset by white cheeks. Both species show a grayish body with varying amounts of white in the wing bars (black-cappeds show an obvious "hockey stick" of white across the wings and an irregular lower edge to the black bib). Carolinas are cleaner looking and slightly smaller. These birds are best separated by range or voice.

SOUNDS
Both species say *chickadee-dee-dee*, but the black-capped's voice is lower and hoarser than the Carolina's. In spring and summer, the Carolina's song is four sweet notes: *fee-bee, fee-bay*. The black-capped's song is two notes: *fee-bee!*

HABITAT
Mixed woodlands with large trees, parks, backyards. In winter both species will join other small songbirds to form mixed-species feeding flocks. These flocks roam across a variety of habitats in search of food.

BACKYARD
Chickadees visit feeders for a variety of foods: sunflower, suet, peanut butter, peanuts, fruit. They use nest boxes for both nesting and roosting and visit birdbaths to bathe and drink.

Carolina Chickadee

Black-capped Chickadee

CAROLINA CHICKADEE

BLACK-CAPPED CHICKADEE

Mountain Chickadee

Poecile gambeli   SIZE: 5¼"

This chickadee, as its name suggests, replaces the black-capped chickadee at higher elevations in the West.

capped chickadee. Song is a series of clear whistled notes, the first one highest: *fee-bee-bee-bee*.

FIELD MARKS
The bold white eyebrow stands out on this chickadee, which is more uniformly gray overall than the black-capped chickadee. Among our chickadees and titmice, only the bridled titmouse (which has a noticeable crest) has a similarly marked face.

HABITAT
Coniferous mountain forests at all seasons. May move to riparian woods at lower elevations in winter.

BACKYARD
Visits feeding stations, particularly in winter, for sunflower seeds and hearts, peanuts, suet, and suet dough.

SOUNDS
Chicka-dee-dee-dee call is hoarser than that of the black-

Chestnut-backed Chickadee

Poecile rufescens   SIZE: 4¾"

This chickadee is a common year-round resident of the northwesternmost portions of North America. It often forages in treetops.

FIELD MARKS
This bird looks like a small black-capped chickadee wearing a chestnut-colored sweater. Its rump is also rusty. Birds along the central coast of California lack the chestnut wash on the sides.

SOUNDS
Call is faster and hoarser than that of the black-capped chickadee: *zick-a-dee-dee.*

HABITAT
Common in both coniferous and deciduous woodlands and in wooded parks.

BACKYARD
An avid visitor to feeding stations for both seeds and suet. Will use nest boxes for nesting.

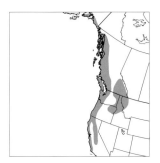

Oak Titmouse

Baeolophus inornatus　　SIZE: 5¾"

Juniper Titmouse

Baeolophus ridgwayi　　SIZE: 5¾"

These two plain-looking titmice were formerly considered a single species (plain titmouse) but now are distinct species, identified most easily by their ranges. The oak titmouse is the only titmouse west of the Sierra Nevada range. The juniper titmouse occurs inland throughout much of the Southwest.

FIELD MARKS
Titmice are plain gray, crested birds with large black eyes and a pale belly. Juniper titmice are slightly grayer, oak titmice slightly browner. Range is the best field mark for identification.

SOUNDS
Oak: song is *wheeti-wheeti-wheeti.* Call is *see-chee.*
Juniper: song is less melodic than Oak's: *tiititi, tiiti ti tiititi.* Call is *see-di-di-di-di.*

HABITAT
Oak: Woods dominated by oaks, riparian woodlands, backyards, and gardens.
Juniper: Woods dominated by junipers, but also found in pinyon and oak woods.

BACKYARD
Both species visit feeders for sunflower seed and hearts, suet and suet dough, peanuts, and mealworms. Both will use nest boxes properly placed in appropriate habitat.

Oak Titmouse

Juniper Titmouse

OAK TITMOUSE

JUNIPER TITMOUSE

Tufted Titmouse

Baeolophus bicolor   SIZE: 6¼"

In the eastern United States and parts of southeastern Canada, the tufted titmouse may be the most avid visitor to bird-feeding stations. Along with the chickadees, this resident species boldly investigates newly placed feeders, becoming one of the first wild birds to key in on a new food source.

FIELD MARKS
The tufted titmouse is gray overall and paler below with a crested head. It has a dark eye on a plain face and buffy flanks.

SOUNDS
Song is *peter-peter-peter.* Also utters a variety of call notes and scolds.

HABITAT
Deciduous woods, parks, woodlots, and backyards.

BACKYARD
Titmice visit feeders for sunflower seed and hearts, peanut butter, peanut bits, and suet and suet dough. They also visit water features to drink and bathe. They may use nest boxes placed in appropriate habitat.

Bushtit

Psaltriparus minimus   SIZE: 4½"

This tiny, nondescript bird spends most of its time on the move, foraging in small mixed-species flocks and looking for insects in shrubs, bushes, and trees.

FIELD MARKS
The bushtit is drab gray overall with a long tail and a tiny black bill. Females have yellow eyes, males black. Pacific Coast birds have a plain face and a brown cap. Interior West birds have a darker brown face and a gray cap. The similar verdin has a yellow head; the wrentit is larger and darker overall.

SOUNDS
Utters soft *seet, pit* notes almost constantly as it forages with flockmates.

HABITAT
Scrubby brushland, mixed woods, woodland edges, well-vegetated residential areas.

BACKYARD
Foraging flocks move through backyards and gardens seeking insects. They visit feeders occasionally for seeds, fruit bits, peanut bits, suet dough, and water.

Adult female

White-breasted Nuthatch

Sitta carolinensis   SIZE: 5¾"

Nuthatches climb around on trees gleaning insects from bark and using their chisel-like bills to open seeds and nuts which they wedge into bark crevices. The white-breasted is the most common backyard visitor among our nuthatches.

FIELD MARKS
As its name suggests, the white-breasted nuthatch is white below. Its back is solid gray. Its face is also white, with a black crown and nape. The smaller but similar red-breasted nuthatch has a white eyebrow, black eye line, and rusty breast and belly.

SOUNDS
Song is a rapid series of nasal *ank* notes. Call is a single *ank*.

HABITAT
Forests, open mixed woods, orchards, parks, and shade trees in suburban backyards.

BACKYARD
Nuthatches readily visit feeders for sunflower seeds, suet and suet dough, peanuts, peanut butter, mealworms, and fruit bits. They also visit water features to drink and bathe. They may use nest boxes placed in wooded habitat.

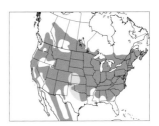

Red-breasted Nuthatch

Sitta canadensis SIZE: 4½"

Red-breasted nuthatches move like tiny wind-up toys along tree branches and trunks and, occasionally, on bird feeders.

FIELD MARKS
This small nuthatch has a black cap, white eyebrow, black eye line, and gray back. Adult males are rusty below. Females and juveniles are paler buff below with paler head markings.

SOUNDS
Nasal, hornlike toots given singly or in a series are higher pitched than the voice of the white-breasted nuthatch. Nuthatches are often heard before they are seen.

HABITAT
Prefers coniferous trees in all seasons but also uses other trees and visits bird feeders.

BACKYARD
In some winters this species moves southward in large numbers, visiting feeders in the southernmost United States. It eats suet, suet dough, peanuts, sunflower seed, mealworms, and peanut butter.

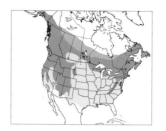

Adult male

Pygmy Nuthatch

Brown-headed
Nuthatch

Pygmy Nuthatch

Sitta pygmaea   SIZE: 4¼"

Brown-headed Nuthatch

Sitta pusilla   SIZE: 4½"

These related species prefer similar habitats (stands of pine trees) but in different places. Both are small gray-backed birds with a brown cap.

FIELD MARKS
Pygmy: brown cap, gray back, buffy white underparts. Brown-headed: similar to pygmy but all white below. They forage by creeping along looking for insects on tree branches and for pine seeds on cones.

SOUNDS
Both species may be heard before they are seen. Pygmy: high-pitched *peep*s in a series. Brown-headed: sounds like a tiny squeak toy: *pee-deedee!*

HABITAT
Pygmy: pine and fir trees. Brown-headed: large stands of pine woods.

BACKYARD
Both species visit backyards in appropriate habitat for suet, suet dough, sunflower hearts, peanut butter, and peanut bits.

PYGMY NUTHATCH

BROWN-HEADED NUTHATCH

Cactus Wren

Campylorhynchus SIZE: 8½"
brunneicapillus

Our largest wren, the cactus wren is a conspicuous bird because of its size, heavily spotted and streaked plumage, and loud, regular vocalizations.

FIELD MARKS
This is a big streaky/spotted wren with a long tail edged in black and white. It has a solid rusty cap and an obvious white eyebrow. The breast is heavily spotted, and the brown back is streaked with white.

SOUNDS
Song is a low-pitched series of hoarse notes on a single tone; sounds more like a scold than a song: *chur-chur-chur-chur*, often speeding up. It is a common bird sound in the desert Southwest.

HABITAT
Arid desert habitat, especially where cactus and mesquite are present.

BACKYARD
Cactus wrens readily forage in backyards with thorny shrub habitat, where they will also build their bulky, football-sized stick nests. They visit water features to drink, and occasionally feeding stations for seed bits.

Carolina Wren

Thryothorus ludovicianus   SIZE: 5½"

Usually heard before it is seen, this wren is a year-round resident throughout its range, where it prefers to live near human habitation.

FIELD MARKS
This wren is rich brown above and warm tan below with a bold white eyebrow and a striped brown tail that is often cocked upward. It is larger than the house wren, the other widespread backyard wren of the East.

SOUNDS
Very vocal year-round. Primary song is a loud, ringing *teakettle, teakettle, teakettle!* Mated pairs stay in contact with a variety of short, musical calls. Scold call is a metallic and harsh *cheerrrrrr-rrr-rrr.*

HABITAT
Brushy thickets and ravines, woodland edges, brushy backyards, and gardens. Regularly nests near humans in garages, sheds, hanging baskets, old cans, etc.

BACKYARD
Visits bird feeders for seed, suet, peanuts, and peanut butter. Also visits birdbaths. Will use nest boxes and any other small enclosed cavity for nesting, especially inside open buildings.

House Wren

Troglodytes aedon SIZE: 4½"

This tiny dark brown woodland and backyard songster is common all across North America in summer. It makes up in voice what it lacks in color. It often holds its tail cocked up at an angle.

FIELD MARKS
The house wren is dark brown above, pale tan below, streaked with darker brown, and has a faint eye line. Both Bewick's and Carolina wrens are larger with bold white eye lines. The winter wren is smaller and rarely comes to backyards.

SOUNDS
Song is a burbling musical trill that rises and then drops in tone. Call is a loud, harsh *purrrr!*

HABITAT
Open woods, woodland edges, wooded parks, gardens, and backyards.

BACKYARD
House wrens are most easily attracted by offering them nest boxes (hence their name) with 1-inch-diameter entrance holes. They will also visit feeders occasionally for suet bits, suet dough, sunflower hearts, and mealworms.

Adult male, crest raised

Ruby-crowned Kinglet

Regulus calendula SIZE: 4¼"

Ruby-crowned kinglets are active birds that constantly flick their wings and hover in place to glean insects from the undersides of leaves.

FIELD MARKS
This drab green bird's tiny size and bold broken eye-ring are good clues to its identity. The male's ruby crown patch is not always visible; it's usually raised only when the male is excited. Females lack the crown patch.

SOUNDS
Song is a thin jumble of musical notes starting with high *tee-tee* phrases and ending with a series of warbled phrases. Call is a distinctive *jee-dit, jee-dit!*

HABITAT
During the breeding season, found in stands of conifers. Other times of year forages in any type of woodland and scrub habitat.

BACKYARD
Though not common visitors to feeders, kinglets may come in for fruit bits, suet or suet dough, mealworms, or peanut bits. They often join winter foraging flocks of chickadees, titmice, and other species.

Eastern Bluebird

Sialia sialis   SIZE: 7"

Bluebirds have a near-mythical status among North Americans because of their beauty, their sweetly musical song, and their willingness to use human-supplied housing. This beloved member of the thrush family has greatly benefited from the efforts of bluebird enthusiasts to provide safe and available nest boxes.

FIELD MARKS
The adult male has a bright blue back, rusty breast, and white belly. The adult female is slightly paler overall. The juvenile is grayish, spotted with white. When perched, bluebirds have a hunch-backed appearance.

SOUNDS
Song is a soft rich warble in short phrases: *tur, tur, turley, turley!* Flight call is a two-noted *ju-lee!* Warning call is a down-slurred *tyew!*

HABITAT
Open grassy habitat, including pastures, grassland, parks, roadsides. Bluebirds are still-hunters—they perch and watch for insects to move below them. They are often seen perching on fences, power lines, and exposed treetops.

BACKYARD
If your backyard is open and grassy, the best way to attract bluebirds is to offer them nest boxes. They will also visit water features to drink and bathe. At feeders they are attracted to suet dough, suet, mealworms, peanut hearts, peanut butter, and fruit bits.

Male

Female

Western Bluebird

Sialia mexicana   SIZE: 7"

The western bluebird is the most richly colored of our three bluebird species. It is found in a variety of open habitats throughout much of the West and is often seen perching on a fencepost, wire, or treetop scanning for its insect prey.

FIELD MARKS

Adult males are deep blue on the head, back, and tail with bright rusty breast, shoulders, and back. The rusty back sets this bluebird apart from the blue-backed eastern and mountain bluebirds. Female westerns are paler overall with a white eye-ring on a grayish face.

SOUNDS

Song is a soft warble: *tew, tew, tewoo.* Call is *tew!*

HABITAT

Open woods, farms, and orchards in spring and summer. In winter, may move to other habitats at lower elevations, including desert mesquite and areas containing berry-bearing plants such as mistletoe and juniper.

BACKYARD

Western bluebirds will use nest boxes placed in appropriate open habitat. They will visit feeders for suet and suet dough, mealworms, and fruit pieces and gardens for winter fruits and berries. They will also visit water features to drink and bathe.

Adult male

Mountain Bluebird

Sialia currucoides   SIZE: 7¼"

Our all-blue bluebird, the mountain bluebird nests in open country at elevations above 5,000 feet in the West. This species often hovers while hunting for insect prey.

FIELD MARKS
The male is sky blue above and light blue below. The female is light blue-gray overall, with darker blue wings. This bluebird is larger and longer-bodied than the western and eastern bluebirds, both of which show some rusty orange in their plumage.

SOUNDS
Song is a soft warbled two-note phrase: *choo-lee*. Call is a thin, descending *wheew!*

HABITAT
Mountain bluebirds nest in open country. They winter in open lowlands with scattered trees. Found in flocks in winter.

BACKYARD
Uses nest boxes in appropriate open habitat. Winter flocks may visit feeding stations for suet, suet dough, fruit bits, and mealworms and for water at birdbaths.

Male

Wood Thrush

Hylocichla mustelina   SIZE: 7¾"

This summer resident of eastern forests has a beautiful song that has enthralled many a poet-naturalist. Wood thrushes only rarely venture out of the deep woods, but their voice carries well beyond their preferred habitat.

FIELD MARKS

This thrush is bright rusty brown on the head, back, and tail with a bright white chest and belly boldly patterned with large dark brown spots. No other thrush has such bold breast markings.

SOUNDS

Song is a flutelike *ee-oh-lay* and similar phrases. Call is *tut-tut-tut.*

HABITAT

Cool and wet deciduous woods in spring and summer. Winters in the Neotropics.

BACKYARD

If your backyard is in the East and is wooded or has old forest nearby, you will hear wood thrushes singing on summer mornings and evenings. They occasionally forage on wooded edges and may visit water features to drink and bathe.

American Robin

Turdus migratorius   SIZE: 10"

You don't have to be a bird watcher to know the American robin. Its brick red breast and dark back are a familiar sight on lawns all across North America. Despite its reputation as a harbinger of spring, many robins spend the winter at northern latitudes, leaving open fields and lawns for the deep woods.

FIELD MARKS
The brick red breast is offset by a black back, head, and tail. The bill is yellow. The dark eye is encircled by a thin white eye-ring. Males are darker backed than females. Young robins leave the nest before they can fly. They are spot-breasted with a bold white eye-ring.

SOUNDS
Song is a rich warble: *cherrio-churry-lee, cheery-up, churr-lee.* During spring and summer, robins are often the first birds to sing in the morning and the last at night. Alarmed birds give a loud *seee!* The common call is *tut-tut-tut.*

HABITAT
Any kind of open ground is suitable for robins, which prefer to forage for earthworms when they're available. Lawns, parks, open meadows, and muddy fields are all likely places to find robins. When snow and ice cover the ground, robins take to the woods to forage for fruits and berries.

BACKYARD
Robins will visit feeders for fruit (apples, grapes, raisins), but you're more likely to see them on your lawn, where they'll find grubs and earthworms. For this reason, robins are often the unfortunate victims of chemically treated lawns. They will also visit birdbaths.

Adult male

Varied Thrush

Ixoreus naevius   SIZE: 9½"

One look at a varied thrush and you'll know this is no normal robin.

FIELD MARKS
A black mask and orange eye stripe, throat, and wing bars, as well as a black breast-band, help separate this from the more widespread American robin. The male has a bluish hue on his back. The female is duller, browner than the male, and lacks the bold breast-band.

SOUNDS
Song is a long, slightly burry, trilled note followed after a pause by a second, lower note. Call is *chook!*

HABITAT
In spring and summer, varied thrushes are found in older, wet coniferous and mixed forests. In fall and winter, they can be found in a variety of habitats, from forest to thickets, parks, and gardens.

They may join winter flocks of American robins.

BACKYARD
Wintering varied thrushes will visit bird feeders for fruit, mealworms, suet and suet dough, and small seed bits. Fruit-bearing plants are especially attractive to this species. They will also visit water features.

Adult male

Gray Catbird

Dumetella carolinensis   SIZE: 8¾"

For a bird that mews like a cat and is gray overall, the gray catbird is well named. This common and widespread bird prefers thickets and is often seen before it is heard.

FIELD MARKS
Only the dark cap and tail and chestnut undertail break up the catbird's overall gray coloration. Its bill, eyes, and legs are dark too.

SOUNDS
Call is a catlike *meww!* Song is a jumble of phrases, some sweet, some nasal, without any regular repetition.

Other common mimics (brown thrasher, northern mockingbird) repeat phrases in their songs.

HABITAT
Thick tangles and underbrush, also woodland edges.

BACKYARD
Catbirds will forage and nest in dense hedgerows and shrubs. They visit backyards for fruiting trees and plants and for water at birdbaths. They occasionally take fruit bits and suet dough from feeders.

Northern Mockingbird

Mimus polyglottos   SIZE: 10"

Our most prolific mimic and singer, the northern mockingbird makes itself conspicuous with its loud and varied song, territorial ways, and the flashes of white in its wings and tail when it flies. It regularly attacks other birds and humans, as well as cats and other predators that cross its territory. It also defends its winter food sources.

FIELD MARKS

The mockingbird is drab gray overall, darker on its back, with obvious white wing patches and outer tail feathers. It is longer billed, lighter colored, and more horizontal in perching posture than the similar loggerhead shrike.

SOUNDS

Imitates other birds, whistles, telephones, barking dogs, and many other sounds in a series, with each phrase repeated more than two times. Young unmated males will sing at night in spring and summer. Call is a harsh *chak!* or a nasal *shairrr!*

HABITAT

Mockingbirds are often found near human habitation, including parks, gardens, farmyards, and brushy thickets along roadways. Ornamental fruit and berry-bearing trees and shrubs are often the center of a wintering mockingbird's territory.

BACKYARD

Mockers will visit feeders for fruit, mealworms, suet, and suet dough. They may be bullies, chasing off other feeder visitors.

European Starling

Sturnus vulgaris   SIZE: 8½"

An introduced species that spread from New York City starting in the late nineteenth century, the European starling now thrives all across North America. It feeds by probing for grubs in soil with its slender bill.

FIELD MARKS

Breeding adults are glossy black with some iridescence in the pale-tipped feathers. Winter birds are dark, spangled with white spots. In flight, starlings look pot-bellied, and their wings look triangular.

SOUNDS

Starlings are vocal masters, able to imitate other birds as well as mechanical sounds such as sirens, telephone rings, and car horns. Primary song is a high-pitched jumble of whistles, whirrs, squeaks, and chatter. Alarm call is a loud *pink! pink! pink!*

HABITAT

Any habitat from rural farmyards to urban sidewalks and shopping malls. Starlings are incredibly common in city parks. In winter they form large foraging flocks that may dominate feeders during bad weather.

BACKYARD

Starlings visit feeders for any food available. Many people spend lots of time and effort attempting to foil starlings from emptying feeders. They also forage in lawns and gardens, removing harmful insects.

Breeding plumage

Cedar Waxwing

Bombycilla cedrorum   SIZE: 7¼"

This is the smaller, more widespread of our two waxwing species. Cedar waxwings are most often found in flocks, which roam far and wide seeking fruit-bearing trees.

FIELD MARKS
The cedar waxwing is warm brown overall with a black mask, a crest (which may be raised or lowered), a bright yellow tail tip, and red waxy tips on its wings (for which the species is named). Juveniles are streaky overall. The larger

Bohemian waxwing has a burnt orange undertail and more white in the wings.

SOUNDS
Call is a high, reedy *tseeee*. Flocks give this call almost constantly.

HABITAT
In spring and summer, open forests, parks, orchards, and in trees near water over which the birds hawk insects. In winter, fruit-bearing trees and shrubs, including ornamental plantings in residential areas.

BACKYARD
Will visit fruiting trees or shrubs in any season. Also attracted to water features and birdbaths. Does not typically visit feeders.

Orange-crowned Warbler

Oreothlypis celata   SIZE: 5"

This warbler is more common in the West than in the East. Its drab overall color can make it difficult to identify.

FIELD MARKS
The color of the upperparts can vary from yellowish to olive-gray, usually paler below. The orange crown is very hard to see. The yellow undertail feathers and the blurry streaks on the breast are the best field marks for this species.

SOUNDS
Song is a weak trill that rises and then descends in tone and fades in volume.

HABITAT
Woodland edges, brushy woods, shrubs, parks, and gardens. Often forages low in vegetation, unlike many other warblers.

BACKYARD
This warbler may forage for insects on backyard or garden vegetation. It will visit feeders for seeds, fruit, peanut butter, suet, and suet dough, and water features for drinking or bathing. It sometimes visits hummingbird feeders for nectar.

Male, breeding plumage

Yellow-rumped Warbler

Dendroica coronata SIZE: 5½"

The yellow-rumped warbler was formerly considered two separate species: "Myrtle" warbler in the East and "Audubon's" warbler in the West. Western birds have a yellow throat, eastern birds a white throat. An active, hardy warbler, the yellow-rumped can change its diet to survive winter weather.

FIELD MARKS
Breeding-plumage males have a black mask, yellow crown, blue-gray back, and a white (East) or yellow (West) throat. Nonbreeding males look like females, but all yellow-rumps retain the yellow rump patch in all plumages.

SOUNDS
Song is a wimpy, two-part trill, similar to that of a junco. Call is a more distinctive *tchup!*

HABITAT
The yellow-rump breeds in coniferous forests. From fall through late spring it can be found in almost any habitat: mixed woods, woodland edges, brushy old-fields, shrubby coastal dunes, parks, gardens, and backyards.

BACKYARD
Migrants can pass through almost any backyard in spring or fall. They may visit bird feeders for sunflower or peanut bits, suet or suet dough, and fruit, or for nectar at hummingbird feeders. They will also visit water features to drink and bathe.

Adult, fall

Black-throated Gray Warbler

Dendroica nigrescens   SIZE: 5"

This warbler is dark above and white below with a boldly marked black-and-white head. It suggests the black-and-white warbler of the East but does not share that species' habit of crawling along branches like a nuthatch.

FIELD MARKS
The black head of the male black-throated gray is intersected with stripes of white. The small yellow lore spot between the eye and bill is more noticeable on males. Females share the dark face but have a white (not black) throat.

SOUNDS
Song is a buzzy series of notes with the accent on the last or next-to-last syllable: *weezy-weezy-weezy-WEETzee.*

HABITAT
Dry mixed woodlands, chaparral, and brushlands.

BACKYARD
Will visit feeders for suet, suet dough, peanut bits, peanut butter, and fruit. Also visits birdbaths.

Male

Summer Tanager

Piranga rubra   SIZE: 7¾"

The summer tanager's large bill is perfect for seizing and killing bees and wasps, which make up much of this species' diet. The birds catch these insects both in flight and by ripping into hives and nests. Summer tanagers are common across the southern and southeastern United States during, you guessed it: summer.

FIELD MARKS
This bird is rose red overall (less bright than the scarlet tanager and without black wings and tail) with a stout pale bill. Females are lemon yellow overall, lacking the darker wings of the female scarlet tanager.

SOUNDS
Song is similar to that of the American robin but slightly hoarser sounding. Call is often heard: *perky-tuck! Perky-tuck-tuck!*

HABITAT
In the East and Southeast, prefers pine-oak woodlands. In the West, found in cottonwoods and in riparian areas.

BACKYARD
Summer tanagers will visit feeders for suet and suet dough, for fruit, and for mealworms, but they are more likely to be seen foraging in large backyard trees or visiting birdbaths.

Male, breeding plumage

Adult female

Scarlet Tanager

Piranga olivacea   SIZE: 7"

The breeding-plumage adult male scarlet tanager is hard to confuse with any other species, but in fall he loses his scarlet plumage, retaining only the black wings and tail. This treetop singer is often heard before it is seen, despite its brilliant coloration.

FIELD MARKS
The breeding male is bright red with black wings and tail and a pale bill. Females and nonbreeding males are yellow-green overall, but males have darker wings. Similar species include the all-red summer tanager of the South and Southwest and the western tanager, which has a red head and yellow body.

SOUNDS
Song sounds like a sore-throated American robin: *churry-cheery-churry-cheery.* Call is a *chip-burr.*

HABITAT
Mixed woodlands, especially oaks, large shade trees, and forested parks.

BACKYARD
Scarlet tanagers might be most attracted to birdbaths, especially if they have moving water. They will also visit feeders for fruit, suet dough, and mealworms, but this is uncommon.

Adult male, breeding plumage

Adult male, nonbreeding plumage

Male, breeding plumage

Adult female

Western Tanager

Piranga ludoviciana

SIZE: 7¼"

The strikingly marked male western tanager is hard to confuse with any other bird. This species spends summers in the coniferous forests of the West and winters in the Neotropics.

FIELD MARKS

Both sexes show bold yellow and white wing bars, a key field mark for this species (no other tanager has wing bars). Breeding adult males have a bright orange-red head and a boldly contrasting yellow and black body, wings, and tail. Fall and winter males are yellow overall with black wings and tail. Some retain a little red on the face. A stout, pale bill helps separate this tanager from orioles.

SOUNDS

Song consists of short, hoarse phrases similar to those of the American robin but less musical. Call is a distinctive *pre-tee-tee!*

HABITAT

Conifer-covered mountains and mixed forests in summer, other wooded habitats in migration.

BACKYARD

The western tanager may pass through your yard in migration, foraging high in the trees. It may visit feeders for fruit bits or take nectar at hummingbird feeders. It may also visit water features to drink or bathe.

Green-tailed Towhee

Pipilo chlorurus   SIZE: 7¼"

Our smallest towhee, the green-tailed has an olive-green back and tail. In summer it is common in wooded mountain habitat. In winter it retreats southward.

FIELD MARKS
The rusty crown, white throat, and black mustache stand out on this olive and gray bird. Its chest is gray, and its belly is dull white. Sexes similar.

SOUNDS
Song starts with two or more whistled notes, followed by a burry trill: *weet-churr chee-chee-chee.* Call is a catlike *mew!*

HABITAT
Thick underbrush of wooded mountain slopes, desert sage, and brushy chaparral.

BACKYARD
May visit feeders near appropriate habitat for mixed seed scattered on the ground.

Spotted Towhee: adult male

Eastern Towhee: adult male

Spotted Towhee

Pipilo maculates SIZE: 8"

Eastern Towhee

Pipilo erythrophthalmus SIZE: 8"

Our two bright orange, black, and white towhees were once considered a single species: the rufous-sided towhee. Now the dark-backed eastern birds are called eastern towhee, and the white-spotted-backed western birds are called spotted towhee.

FIELD MARKS
Males of both species have a bold black head, red eyes, a rufous belly, and a long black tail edged in white. Females are browner versions of the males. The dark back of the spotted towhee is covered in white spots, for which the species is named. Both species are ground-loving birds that make their living scratching through the leaf litter for food.

SOUNDS
Eastern towhee song: *drink-your-teeeeee!* Call: *chew-ink!* Spotted towhee song: *Cheeeeeeee!* Call: a nasal *cheweee!*

HABITAT
Open woods, brushy areas, woodland edges, hedgerows, gardens, and bird feeders.

BACKYARD
Both towhee species will visit feeders for seed scattered on the ground, especially mixed seed, cracked corn, and millet. They will also visit birdbaths to drink and bathe.

SPOTTED TOWHEE

EASTERN TOWHEE

Canyon Towhee

Melozone fuscus   SIZE: 8¾"

California Towhee

Melozone crissalis   SIZE: 9"

These two drab brown, ground-loving birds were once considered a single species. Canyon towhee is the more inland-dwelling species. California towhee, as its name suggests, is found in the western half of California.

FIELD MARKS
Their overall plainness and long tail are the best field marks for these birds. California towhees are darker overall with a pale rusty throat. Canyon towhees have a rusty cap. Both birds can best be separated by range.

SOUNDS
California: song is a rapid series on a single note: *chink-chink-chink-tinktinktinktink*. Canyon: song is a series of two-syllable notes, speeding up: *shidip-shidip-shidipshidipshidip*.

HABITAT
Brushy areas, scrublands, canyons, parks, gardens, thickly vegetated residential backyards.

BACKYARD
Both species readily visit feeding stations for mixed seed scattered on the ground.

Canyon Towhee

California Towhee

CANYON TOWHEE

CALIFORNIA TOWHEE

Chipping Sparrow

Spizella passerina SIZE: 5½"

Often overlooked because of its nonmusical song and small size, the "chippie" is one of our most common sparrows.

FIELD MARKS
Slender and flat-headed, with a plain gray breast and a long tail, the male has an obvious rusty cap in breeding plumage. In fall (nonbreeding plumage), adults appear streaky-capped with a dull gray eye line. Several similar-looking (and closely related) sparrows also visit backyards and feeding stations, including the tree sparrow, field sparrow, and clay-colored sparrow.

SOUNDS
Song is a long, dry trill on a single pitch. Call is a thin *seet*.

HABITAT
Young woodlands and woodland edges, pines, farms, orchards, gardens, and landscaped suburban backyards.

BACKYARD
A common feeder visitor, except when insects are abundantly available. Prefers mixed seed and cracked corn scattered on the ground or in low platform feeders. Visits water features and often nests in low shrubbery in gardens, parks, and backyards.

Breeding plumage

Field Sparrow

Spizella pusilla   SIZE: 5¾"

A plain-faced sparrow of grassy meadows and shrubby fields of the eastern half of the continent, the field sparrow is often heard before it is seen.

FIELD MARKS

The field sparrow has a pink bill and a black eye with a faint white eye-ring, and its head and back are washed with warm brown. Its breast is plain. The wings show two indistinct white wing bars. The similar tree sparrow shows a black central breast spot. The chipping sparrow has a bright white eye line.

SOUNDS

Song is a long series of sweet notes, descending in tone but gaining in speed. The pattern of notes is like a ball bouncing to a stop. Call is *tsew!* Males often sing all day in summer and may sing on moonlit nights.

HABITAT

Old meadows with scattered brush or saplings. Grassy woodland edges.

BACKYARD

Readily visits bird feeders in rural settings for mixed seed, sunflower hearts or bits, suet dough, and cracked corn. Also visits water features.

Fox Sparrow

Passerella iliaca   SIZE: 7"

This is a large, plump-looking, boldly marked sparrow that occurs in several color variations: a rusty one in the East and North and darker, grayer birds in the West. It forages by scratching at ground litter with its large feet to uncover seeds and other food items.

FIELD MARKS

Most fox sparrows show a rusty rump and tail. Eastern birds are fox red. They look large-billed and are more boldly marked on the breast than other sparrows. They are much stockier than the similar song sparrow.

SOUNDS

Song is lovely series of clear whistled notes, more finchlike than sparrowlike: *sweet-sweet, chee-chee-chee-titititi-chew-wee.* Call is a loud *chip!*

HABITAT

Dense underbrush, thick woodlands, hedgerows. Except for males singing during courtship, this species spends much of its time on or near the ground.

BACKYARD

Visits feeders to scratch for seed fallen on the ground. May prefer to forage in nearby undergrowth if feeders are in an open area.

Eastern adult

Song Sparrow

Melospiza melodia   SIZE: 6¼"

A common backyard bird across most of North America, the song sparrow is equally happy living in a suburban backyard or along the edge of a remote forest. It is named for its pleasing song, which it sings regularly throughout the spring, summer, and fall.

FIELD MARKS

The song sparrow is medium sized with a long round-tipped tail and a heavily streaked breast with a central breast spot. This species varies quite a bit in color and size, from the pale eastern birds to the darker western birds.

SOUNDS

Song is a series of musical notes with a few buzzy tones interspersed. It typically starts with three or four clear notes: *sweet-sweet-sweet . . .*

HABITAT

Brushy habitat, thickets, woodland edges, old meadows, gardens, parks, and shrubbery.

BACKYARD

Song sparrows will scratch for seed bits below your bird feeder. They will also eat sunflower bits, peanut bits, and suet dough from a low platform feeder. They visit water features to drink and bathe.

Lincoln's Sparrow

Melospiza lincolnii   SIZE: 5¾"

Lincoln's sparrow is similar to the more common song sparrow but is more finely marked, with a gray face and buffy chest. It nests across the northern tier of North America and in western mountain bogs, and winters in the southernmost states. It is most commonly seen in migration.

FIELD MARKS
A finely marked sparrow with a gray face and buffy chest, Lincoln's has fine brown streaks on its chest and sides. A slight white eye-ring stands out on a darkish face.

SOUNDS
Song resembles that of the house wren in tone. It consists of two introductory notes followed by a warbled phrase or two, rising and then falling in a nasal buzz at the end. Call is *bseeet!*

HABITAT
Breeds in wet wooded thickets of alder and willow and in boggy meadows. Winters in brushy habitat, thickets, and yards or gardens with heavy underbrush or hedgerows.

BACKYARD
May visit feeders for mixed seed.

White-throated Sparrow

Zonotrichia albicollis   SIZE: 6¾"

White-throated sparrows nest in the far North and mountain West. They are common in all seasons in much of the West. In the East, they are commonly seen in backyards from fall through early spring.

FIELD MARKS
The stripes on the head can be black and white or tan and buff. The throat is bright white. The yellow lore spot in front of the eye is a key field mark. The bill is dark, the breast and belly gray. The white-throat's posture is less erect than that of the "taller-looking" white-crowned sparrow.

SOUNDS
Song is *old Sam Peabody, Peabody, Peabody.* Call is *tseet!*

HABITAT
Brambles, shrubby woodlands, forest edges, old-fields, brushy gardens, and backyards.

BACKYARD
The white-throated sparrow is a regular feeder visitor for mixed seed scattered on the ground or on low platform feeders. It also visits water features.

Harris's Sparrow

Zonotrichia querula   SIZE: 7½"

This large sparrow has a pink bill that stands out against a black forehead and bib. Most bird watchers see this sparrow only in winter, which it spends in the southcentral United States. It nests at the edge of the boreal forest in the far north.

FIELD MARKS
The black bib, pink bill, and large size are the best field marks. The amount of black can vary widely. The face is tan, the back is tan on brown, and the belly is white.

SOUNDS
Song is a series of sweet, quavering whistles on two tones. Call is *tink*.

HABITAT
Breeds in the far North, at the edge of the tree line. In winter, found in hedgerows, brushy field edges, open woods, and at bird feeders.

BACKYARD
Harris's sparrows will forage beneath bird feeders for seed bits. They are often found in mixed flocks with white-crowned sparrows.

Breeding plumage

White-crowned Sparrow

Zonotrichia leucophrys   SIZE: 7"

The white-crowned sparrow is aptly named and regularly associates with other sparrows in mixed flocks.

FIELD MARKS
Bold black and white stripes on the head of adults, combined with a gray throat and pinkish bill, separate this sparrow from the similar white-throated sparrow. The back is brown, streaked with black. The wings show two slight wing bars. Immature birds have a tan-striped head.

SOUNDS
Song is one or two clear musical notes followed by a trilled whistle, similar to that of the white-throated sparrow. Call is a sharp *pink!*

HABITAT
Forest edges, brushy tangles, grassland, chaparral, roadsides, and shrubby backyards.

BACKYARD
Will visit feeders in fall and winter for mixed seed scattered on the ground. Will also visit water features.

Adult

Golden-crowned Sparrow

Zonotrichia atricapilla   SIZE: 7¼"

The golden crown outlined in black gives this sparrow its name. It nests in western Canada and Alaska, so most bird watchers see it in winter when it often forms mixed flocks with white-crowned sparrows.

FIELD MARKS
Breeding birds show a bold gold and black crown. This fades in winter but is still a useful field mark. The back is brownish with dark streaks, and the breast and belly are pale gray-brown. The bill is dull gray.

SOUNDS
A hoarse three-note call, descending in tone: *oh DEAR me!* May sing in winter on sunny days.

HABITAT
Breeds in boreal and alpine habitats. Winters in shrubby tangles, hedgerows, woodlands, chaparral, and areas of dense undergrowth.

BACKYARD
Will visit platform feeders for mixed seed, millet, sunflower bits, and other foods. Often forages on the ground beneath feeders. Also visits water features to bathe and drink.

Dark-eyed Junco

Junco hyemalis   SIZE: 6½"

This member of the sparrow family is dark above and white below, like the winter sky and landscape, the season during which juncos visit most of our backyards. There are six different "forms" of the dark-eyed junco, mostly in the West. Several of these were once considered separate species.

FIELD MARKS
All forms of the junco show a dark hood and, in flight, white outer tail feathers. Most show a dark gray or gray and brown back, dark eye, pale bill, and white belly. Flanks may be gray, buffy, or pale pink.

SOUNDS
Song is a loose, musical trill on a single pitch: *tiitiitiitiitiitii,* similar to a chipping sparrow song. May sing on sunny winter days. Call is a sharp *tick!*

HABITAT
Frequents deciduous or mixed coniferous woods during the breeding season. In the nonbreeding season, found in old fields, brushy roadsides, along woodland edges, in parks and gardens, and at feeding stations. Often found in flocks in winter.

BACKYARD
Juncos prefer mixed seed or cracked corn at feeders but will also eat suet dough offered in a low feeder or scattered on the ground. They regularly forage in weedy patches and winter-killed gardens.

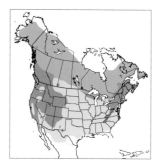

Adult male

Adult male

Adult female

Northern Cardinal

Cardinalis cardinalis   SIZE: 8¾"

The male cardinal is hard to mistake for any other species. It is our only all-red bird with a prominent crest. It's a common year-round resident of the eastern United States and southernmost Canada, as well as the desert Southwest to Arizona.

FIELD MARKS
Adult males are bright red with a red crest, black face, and orange-pink bill. Adult females are rosy brown overall with a red-tipped crest, black face, and pale pink bill. Juveniles are all brown with a dark gray bill.

SOUNDS
Song is loud and variable series of whistled notes: *sweet-CHEER CHEER CHEER!* Or *purty-purty-purty.* Call is a loud, metallic *teek!*

HABITAT
Open woods, woodland edges, farmyards, parks, and backyards and gardens with thick brush.

BACKYARD
Readily visits feeders for sunflower seeds, peanuts, suet dough, and mealworms. Also visits water features to bathe and drink.

Pyrrhuloxia

Cardinalis
sinuatus

SIZE: 8¾"

Nicknamed the "desert cardinal" for its resemblance to the northern cardinal, the pyrrhuloxia has only patches of red on its overall gray body. It is a resident bird from south Texas west to Arizona.

FIELD MARKS
The male has a wash of red on the face, crest tip, and breast and belly. His crest is long, and his bill is large and yellow. Females are dull gray overall with a hint of red on the crest and chest.

SOUNDS
A very cardinal-like series of two-note phrases: *chee-doo-chee-doo.* Call is a metallic *chik!*

HABITAT
Desert scrub, thickets, and brushy areas, often near water.

BACKYARD
Pyrrhuloxias will visit feeders for mixed seed, millet, sunflower, peanuts, suet, fruit, and nuts. They visit water features to drink and bathe.

Rose-breasted Grosbeak

Pheucticus ludovicianus

SIZE: 8"

A medium-sized songbird with a large seed-crushing bill, the rose-breasted grosbeak spends the breeding season in deciduous woods across the northern portions of North America. It winters in the Neotropics.

FIELD MARKS

Adult males in breeding plumage show an obvious rose-colored V on the breast. The head, back, wings, and tail are mostly black. The wing bars, flanks, and rump are bright white. Females and young birds are streaked with brown, like an oversized female purple finch.

SOUNDS

Song is a series of rich, warbled phrases, similar to that of the American robin. Call is *eek!*, like a tennis shoe squeaking on a gym floor. This note is often the first clue to this species' presence.

HABITAT

Deciduous woods, parks, and orchards. Visits feeders in spring and summer.

BACKYARD

Grosbeaks eat black-oil and striped sunflower seeds at feeders. They also visit water features to drink and bathe.

Male, breeding plumage

Juvenile male, fall

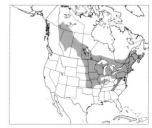

Black-headed Grosbeak

Pheucticus melanocephalus

SIZE: 8¼"

As its name suggests, the chunky-looking black-headed grosbeak has a big powerful bill perfectly designed for cracking seeds. Breeding-plumaged males are boldly marked with orange, black, and white.

FIELD MARKS
Adult males in breeding plumage have a black head, orange body, black tail, and black wings with bold white wing bars. Females and immatures show a buffy breast and streaky back. Flying birds show yellow wing linings. Males in nonbreeding plumage lack the all-black head.

SOUNDS
Song is a series of musical phrases, rising and falling—similar to the song of the American robin. Call is a loud, sharp *eek!*

HABITAT
Woodlands and woodland edges.

BACKYARD
Visits backyard feeding stations for all types of sunflower seed.

Adult female

Male, breeding plumage

Adult female

Male, breeding plumage

Indigo Bunting

Passerina cyanea SIZE: 5½"

The indigo bunting is a blue songbird common across the eastern two-thirds of the United States and southernmost Canada. Males are often seen singing from a treetop perch from spring through late summer.

FIELD MARKS
The adult male in breeding plumage is deep blue overall with a silver bill and black wings and tail suffused with blue. Adult females are drab brown overall. Winter and molting males are brown with a hint of blue on the wings, rump, and tail. Indigos often switch their tail back and forth while foraging.

SOUNDS
Song is a series of loud, ringing notes in pairs, descending in tone: *Fire-fire, where-where? There-there, put it out.* Call is a diagnostic *spit!*

HABITAT
Brushy woodland edges, old-fields, and woodland clearings.

BACKYARD
Indigo buntings will visit feeders for sunflower bits and mixed seed, especially in spring migration. They use water features for bathing and drinking.

Painted Bunting

Passerina ciris   SIZE: 5½"

The painted bunting is North America's most colorful bird. It's a shame its range is so limited. Within its range, this species is locally common.

FIELD MARKS
The gaudy adult male has a blue head, red eye-ring, bright yellow back, and brilliant red throat, chest, belly, and rump. The adult female is our only all-green bird.

SOUNDS
Song is a series of buzzy warbled notes. Call is a sharp *chip*.

HABITAT
Prefers thickets, tangled underbrush, and woodland edges.

BACKYARD
Painted buntings will come to feeders for mixed seed and sunflower bits. They visit water features to drink and bathe.

Adult female

Adult male

Red-winged Blackbird

Agelaius phoeniceus   SIZE: 8¾"

For many bird watchers the appearance of red-winged blackbirds is a more reliable sign of spring than the appearance of American robins. Male red-wings often return to set up territories before the snow has melted in the North. They are associated with wet areas, swamps, and cattail marshes.

FIELD MARKS
Males of this medium-sized species are glossy black with bright red shoulder patches edged in yellow. Females and young birds are streaky brown overall and can be confused with sparrows.

SOUNDS
The male's territorial song is a loud, ringing *conk-a-ree!* As he sings, he puffs up and flares his red shoulder patches. Call, often given in flight, is a loud *chack!*

HABITAT
Marshes, ponds, wet meadows, and cattail stands. Blackbirds forage in these habitats and in nearby farm fields. In winter they gather in large flocks, often with other blackbird species.

BACKYARD
Will visit feeders in any season for cracked corn, sunflower bits, suet dough, and fruit. Flocks may visit feeders in winter when snow and ice make foraging difficult.

Adult male

Adult female

Yellow-headed Blackbird

Xanthocephalus SIZE: 9½"
xanthocephalus

This common summer resident nests in loose colonies in marshes and wet fields of the Midwest and West. In winter it joins large blackbird flocks and moves south.

FIELD MARKS
The adult male has a hood of mustard yellow, a black body, and bold white wing patches. Females are brown overall with a pale yellow throat.

SOUNDS
Male's "song" is a low, hoarse, retching sound sung from an obvious perch in his territory. Call is *chack!*

HABITAT
Marshes with cattails, wet fields, and lakeshores. Forages in farm fields and in feedlots.

BACKYARD
Yellow-headed blackbirds are more likely to visit feeders in migration and in winter, when they often associate with mixed-species flocks of other blackbirds. They eat cracked corn and other seeds and grains scattered on the ground. They may also visit water features.

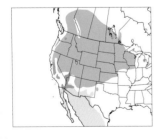

Adult male

Adult female

Rusty Blackbird

Euphagus carolinus   SIZE: 9"

Named for its rusty-colored fall plumage, the rusty blackbird nests in the wet boreal woods and bogs of the North. In winter it comes south in mixed blackbird flocks. Populations are rapidly declining because of habitat loss and other environmental factors.

FIELD MARKS
The rusty blackbird is smaller than a common grackle but larger than a brown-headed cowbird. With its pale eye and longish slender bill, it is similar to the Brewer's blackbird (which has a shorter bill and does not take on a rusty fall plumage). If you see a blackbird foraging on the ground in the woods, it's likely to be a rusty blackbird.

SOUNDS
Song is a harsh *cush-a-ree*, like a rusty door hinge opening. Call is *chack!*

HABITAT
Wet woods, riparian woods, wooded swamps, pond edges, and bogs.

BACKYARD
Rusty blackbirds may visit feeders for mixed seed, cracked corn, and sunflower bits, usually in the company of other blackbird species. They forage on the ground.

Male, breeding plumage

Brewer's Blackbird

Euphagus cyanocephalus   SIZE: 9"

This is the common blackbird of the West, found in all kinds of habitats from mountain meadows to shopping malls. Its iridescent all-black plumage and pale eye help separate it from the European starling, brown-headed cowbird, and red-winged blackbird. The similar great-tailed grackle is twice the size of the Brewer's blackbird.

FIELD MARKS

The male is all black with some slight greenish or purple iridescence on the wings and back in bright sunlight. He has a pale eye and a short, thin bill. The female is dark brown with a dark eye and pale eye line.

SOUNDS

Song (if you can call it that) is a harsh, rising *shreee.* Call is a typical blackbird *tchack!*

HABITAT

Found in any open habitat, including parks, parking lots, meadows, farm feedlots, pastures, and fields. Usually forages on the ground.

BACKYARD

Visits backyards for seed scattered on the ground, especially cracked corn, but will also eat any kind of food scraps, plus suet dough, suet, peanut bits, fruit pieces, and sunflower hearts. Mixed flocks of blackbirds often visit feeders during migration and in bad weather.

Adult male

Common Grackle

Quiscalus quiscula   SIZE: 12½"

This long-tailed, pale-eyed bird appears all black. But a closer look at an adult male grackle in bright sunlight reveals iridescent tones of green, gold, and purple in the plumage. Grackles are often found in large flocks in fall and winter.

FIELD MARKS

The male is all dark with a pale eye. The female is lighter and less iridescent. In flight, the adult male holds his tail in a V shape. The long powerful bill is perfect for the grackle's widely varied diet.

SOUNDS

Song is a rasping, grating *krr-zheee!* Call, often given in flight, is a sharp *chack!*

HABITAT

Found in a variety of habitats from backyards, gardens, and parks to farmyards and agricultural fields. Nests colonially in conifer stands. Forages in open, grassy habitat.

BACKYARD

Grackles will eat almost anything offered at a feeder, including cracked corn, nuts, and sunflower hearts. In summer they are known to soften hard food items (bread crusts, dog kibble) in birdbaths. They will also attack, kill, and eat small songbirds and rodents.

Adult male

Great-tailed Grackle

Quiscalus mexicanus   SIZE: 15" (FEMALE) TO 18" (MALE)

Like a supersized common grackle, the great-tailed grackle is a big iridescent black bird common in the southwestern quarter of the United States. It is almost always found in noisy flocks.

FIELD MARKS
The male is a large glossy dark purple bird with a long keel-shaped tail, a large bill, and yellow eyes. The female is brownish overall. This species is similar to the common grackle but much larger.

SOUNDS
Many varied calls, including a harsh *chack-chack-chack!* and a shrill, high-pitched *kee-kee-* *kee!* Also various whistles and discordant notes. Grackles are very vocal in flocks and will call all night in roosts near brightly lit settings.

HABITAT
Farms, fields, feedlots, parks, and parking lots in urban and suburban settings.

BACKYARD
Will visit feeders for seed, fruit, suet, bread, pet food, etc. Visits water features to drink, bathe, and to soften hard food items in water. Grackles are common in areas of heavy human activity, such as malls, shopping centers, and parks.

Adult male

Adult male

Brown-headed Cowbird

Molothrus ater   SIZE: 7½"

This is a compact blackbird with a stout, conical bill. Cowbirds are named for their habit of following and foraging around herds of cattle. To cope with this nomadic lifestyle, cowbirds do not build nests or raise their own young. Instead, they lay their eggs in the nests of other songbirds and leave the parenting to their unwitting hosts.

FIELD MARKS
Males have a black body and a brown head (for which they are named). Females and immatures are drab brown and streaky overall. The stout bill and dark eyes help separate this species from Brewer's and rusty blackbirds, European starling, and the longer-tailed grackles.

SOUNDS
Male's song in spring is a mix of low gurgles and high squeaky whistles. Call is a two-syllabled *tse-tseeeet!*

HABITAT
Open grassy habitats, including pastures, plowed fields, gardens, woodland edges, parks, and backyards.

BACKYARD
Cowbirds love mixed seed and cracked corn scattered on the ground, but they will also eat sunflower seed from tube feeders. Many bird watchers tailor their offerings to discourage this nest parasite in spring and summer. They may form large flocks from fall through early spring.

Adult female

Orchard Oriole

Icterus spurius   SIZE: 7¼"

This dark orange (male) oriole can indeed be found in orchards, but it is also found in brushy areas of all kinds. It is smaller and darker than most of our other orioles, and in bright or very low light it can appear all black.

FIELD MARKS
The adult male is burnt orange on the chest, belly, and rump, with a black hood, back, wings, and tail. Adult females are olive green above and yellow below with faint white wing bars. Immature males are yellow-green with a black throat.

SOUNDS
Song is a series of slurred whistles with a few buzzy notes. Call is a harsh *chack*.

HABITAT
Nests and forages in brushy edge habitat, orchards, parks, and shade trees near water.

BACKYARD
The orchard oriole will forage in backyards with appropriate habitat within its range. It may visit feeders for nectar, grape jelly, fruit, suet dough, and mealworms. It also visits water features.

Adult male

Adult female

Hooded Oriole

Icterus cucullatus   SIZE: 7½"

The hooded oriole has an orange hood—not a black hood as its name might suggest. An orange oriole of the desert Southwest and south Texas, it is often associated with palm trees.

FIELD MARKS
Breeding males are bright orange with a black face and throat and black wings and tail. The similar Bullock's oriole has a black crown, nape, and eye line. The hooded oriole's crown and nape are unmarked bright orange. The female is yellow-orange below and yellow-green above.

SOUNDS
Song is a rapid series of trills and throaty whistles. Call is *eeek!* or *wheek!*

HABITAT
Open woods, palms, shade trees in parks, gardens, and backyards.

BACKYARD
Hooded orioles will visit backyards for nectar at feeders, citrus halves, and water. They prefer to nest in palm trees.

Adult male

Baltimore Oriole

Icterus galbula   SIZE: 8½"

Bullock's Oriole

Icterus bullockii   SIZE: 8½"

These are bright orange and black birds with a slender bill. The range of each species covers about half of North America: Baltimore in the East and Bullock's in the West. These birds were once considered separate forms of a single species.

FIELD MARKS
Males of both species are deep orange. Females have a light gray-buffy body and pale orange head. The male Baltimore has an all-black hood. The male Bullock's has a black cap and throat offset by orange cheeks and large white wing patches on black wings.

SOUNDS
Baltimore: a treetop singer. Beautiful whistled notes in a series: *See me? Here I am! Up here!* He also sings a series of chattery notes.
Bullock's: paired notes in a series. Also a hoarse chatter.

HABITAT
Baltimore: open deciduous woods, parks, and backyards with large shade trees. Bullock's: riparian woods, shade trees in parks and farmyards, woodlots.

BACKYARD
Both species will visit feeders for orange or grapefruit halves and occasionally for suet or suet dough. They're also attracted to nectar at hummingbird feeders and grape jelly at oriole feeders. They will visit birdbaths to bathe and drink.

224

Baltimore Oriole: adult male

Baltimore Oriole: adult female

Bullock's Oriole: adult male

BALTIMORE ORIOLE

BULLOCK'S ORIOLE

Gray-crowned Rosy-Finch

Leucosticte tephrocotis   SIZE: 6–8"

Our three rosy-finch species (gray-crowned, black, and brown-capped) were once considered a single species, rosy finch. Of these, the gray-crowned is the most common and widespread in winter. Rosy-finches are large birds, usually found in noisy mixed flocks.

FIELD MARKS
This dark brown bird has a gray crown and black forehead. The lower belly, wings, and rump are washed with rose pink. The male is more boldly colored than the female. Rosy-finches walk when on the ground foraging. Their flight, like that of other finches, is undulating.

SOUNDS
Call is similar to that of the house sparrow: *cha-DEEP!* Flocks call constantly.

HABITAT
Nests in the far northwest on tundra and at high altitudes. Winters in western mountains, venturing to lower elevations to forage in open fields and at bird feeders.

BACKYARD
In winter in western mountains, visits bird feeders for Nyjer seed and sunflower hearts.

Adult male

Pine Grosbeak

Pinicola enucleator

SIZE: 9"

This species nests in northernmost North America and in the western mountains. Flocks occasionally move far to the south when food is scarce in northern forests.

FIELD MARKS
This large chunky finch (almost robin-sized) has a stout bill and a long notched tail. The male's coloration can vary among individuals from pink to brick red on the head, breast, and rump. Females are gray overall with a wash of lime green or russet on the crown and rump. Both sexes show two white wing bars.

SOUNDS
Song is a melodic warble. Call varies by region. In the West, *chee-vli;* in the East, *tew-tew-tew.*

HABITAT
Pine grosbeaks are often found in conifers and larches. In winter they can be found in fruit trees, deciduous woods, and shade trees. They may forage for salt and grit along roadways.

BACKYARD
Foraging flocks of pine grosbeaks will visit feeders for sunflower seed. Ornamental and fruit trees such as crab apples, plums, and apples are attractive to this species, which is often unwary of humans and can be approached closely.

Adult male

Adult female

Purple Finch

Carpodacus
purpureus

SIZE: 6"

More raspberry colored than purple (male), the purple finch is a common feeder visitor in winter across the eastern parts of the continent and along the Pacific Coast. It nests in the northern boreal forest and at higher elevations in eastern and western mountains.

FIELD MARKS
The male is raspberry red overall with brown wings and tail and a white belly. The female is heavily but cleanly streaked with brown overall. Whereas the male purple finch has an unstreaked chest, belly, and sides, the male house finch is usually more brick red and has obviously streaked sides.

SOUNDS
Song is a musical warble. Call is a loud *pit!*

HABITAT
Wooded habitat, pine groves, parks, and backyard feeding stations.

BACKYARD
Eats sunflower seeds of all kinds, suet dough, peanut bits, and fruit at feeders. Also visits water features to drink and bathe.

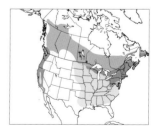

Cassin's Finch

Carpodacus cassinii   SIZE: 6¼"

Cassin's finch is very similar in appearance to its two more common cousins, the purple finch and house finch, but has a more strongly notched tail. It has a stronger preference for mountain forest habitat.

FIELD MARKS
The male Cassin's finch has a red forecrown that is set off by brown at the back of the head. His chest is paler pink than that of the male purple finch's. The female Cassin's is more cleanly marked in brown and white than the female purple or house finch. Cassin's finch has a more elongated bill too.

SOUNDS
Song is similar to, but more musical than, that of the purple finch. Call is three syllables: *giddyup!*

HABITAT
Mountain forests, especially conifers. Moves to lower elevations in winter, when it is more likely to visit feeders.

BACKYARD
Visits feeders for sunflower seeds and hearts, Nyjer seed.

Adult male

Adult male (left) and female

House Finch

Carpodacus mexicanus

SIZE: 6"

Once a bird only of the West, the house finch was introduced to the East in the 1940s and now inhabits the entire continent.

FIELD MARKS
Males have a brick red face, breast, and rump and a streaky brown cap, back, and wings. Females are streaky brown overall. Brown streaks on the male's white belly help separate this species from the male purple finch, which is washed with raspberry red overall and is unstreaked below.

SOUNDS
A loud and happy-sounding song of bright musical notes ending in a down-slurred *where!* Call is a musical *churp!*

HABITAT
Woodland edges in parks, suburbs, and farmlots; especially common near bird feeders.

BACKYARD
House finches eagerly visit feeders for sunflower seeds and hearts, Nyjer seed, peanut bits, and suet dough. A bacterial infection of the eyes has reduced this species' numbers in the East.

Adult male

Red Crossbill

Loxia curvirostra   SIZE: 5¾"–7"

White-winged Crossbill

Loxia leucoptera   SIZE: 6½"

These two similar species share the oddly crossed mandibles for which they are named. These bills are perfect for prying seeds out of pine cones and the seed enclosures of other trees. Crossbills will breed at any time of year if there is enough food in the form of pine seeds.

FIELD MARKS
Crossbills are large chunky finches with heavy, crossed mandibles. Males of both species are red overall, but coloration varies in intensity among individuals. Females are yellow to yellow-green. White-winged crossbills are slightly larger and show obvious white wing bars.

SOUNDS
Red: song is a musical series of warbles and metallic clicks. Call is *jip-jip*.
White-winged: song is a series of trills with loud chip notes interspersed. Call is *chit-chit-chit*.

HABITAT
Crossbills breed and forage in coniferous forests, especially spruce, hemlock, larch, and tamarack. In winter they may range far and wide in search of food.

BACKYARD
Foraging flocks may visit feeders well to the south of the normal wintering range. They eat sunflower seed but are more likely to visit nearby stands of large cone-bearing conifers and to drink at water features.

RED CROSSBILL

WHITE-WINGED CROSSBILL

White-winged Crossbill: adult male

White-winged Crossbill: adult female

Red Crossbill: molting adult male

Common Redpoll

Acanthis flammea   SIZE: 5¼"

The redpoll is named for its red cap (or "poll"), which both males and females show. This northern finch almost always occurs in flocks, which may also include pine siskins, American goldfinches, and purple finches.

FIELD MARKS
This redpoll is streaky brown above and white below. The red forehead, black goatee, and small pale bill are key field marks. Males often show some rosy pink on the upper breast. The tail is noticeably forked.

SOUNDS
Song is a long series of twitters, rising in tone: *chit-chit-chit-chewee!* Call, given in flight, is *che-che-che-che.*

HABITAT
Nests in the far North where the tree line meets the tundra. Flocks come far south in some years, when natural seed crop in the North is diminished. Often found in weedy fields in winter.

BACKYARD
Redpolls are a favorite feeder visitor for many birders because of their infrequent forays southward and their loyalty to well-stocked feeding stations. They especially enjoy Nyjer seed but will also eat sunflower hearts and bits.

Pine Siskin

Spinus pinus   SIZE: 5"

This streaky, slender finch sometimes goes unnoticed when mixed with a winter flock of goldfinches. A closer look reveals yellow patches in the wings and tail that flash when the bird flies. Its distinctive call stands out amid the chatter of goldfinches.

FIELD MARKS
Fine streaking in tones of brown and gray, a thin bill, and a notched tail help set the pine siskin apart from our other common finches, which do not have yellow in the wings and tail. Siskins are very active and often aggressive at bird feeders.

SOUNDS
Song resembles that of the American goldfinch. Calls are more commonly heard, especially from flying siskins. A shrill, rising *zhreee!* is the most distinctive.

HABITAT
Pines and deciduous woods, especially alders, birches, and sweetgum trees, and weedy edge habitat and bird feeders.

BACKYARD
Prefers Nyjer seed but will also eat black-oil sunflower and sunflower hearts. Will visit water features and will also forage for seeds in winter gardens and flower beds.

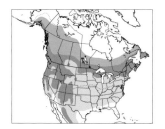

Adult male

Lesser Goldfinch

Spinus psaltria

SIZE: 4½"

This, our smallest goldfinch species, is widespread in the western and southwestern United States. It comes in two subspecies: a black-backed form and a green-backed form. Like other finches, it is often found in flocks.

FIELD MARKS

Males of both subspecies have a black crown and yellow breast and belly. Black-backed males are black from head to tail. Green-backed males are dull olive from nape to rump with a black tail. Both subspecies have white in the black wings.

SOUNDS

Song is similar to that of the American goldfinch but is given in more distinct phrases: *tee-yee, tee-yer.*

HABITAT

Open country, weedy fields, brushy areas along streams, and parks and gardens.

BACKYARD

This goldfinch visits feeders for sunflower seeds and hearts and Nyjer seed. It also visits water features to bathe and drink.

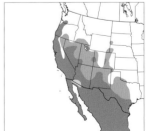

American Goldfinch

Spinus tristis SIZE: 5"

The folk name for the goldfinch says it all: wild canary. From spring through late fall, male goldfinches are brilliant canary yellow, black, and white. But they lose these colors for the winter, when they look so dull greenish gray that many people wonder where their goldfinches have gone.

FIELD MARKS
Spring and summer males are boldly marked with a yellow body, black face and wings, and white wing bars. Females are duller overall but show blacker wings in spring and summer. Winter males resemble females.

SOUNDS
Like canaries, American goldfinches are avid singers, uttering a rich warbling series of musical twitters. In flight they give a distinctive rhythmic call: *potato-chip, potato-chip*.

HABITAT
Forages in flocks all year long, searching for seeds and buds in brushy habitat, overgrown meadows, and along woodland edges.

BACKYARD
Visits backyards for sunflower and Nyjer seeds at bird feeders and for water at birdbaths. Seed-producing flowering plants such as sunflowers, coneflowers, and zinnias are also favorites of goldfinches.

Nonbreeding

Adult male

Evening Grosbeak

Coccothraustes vespertinus   SIZE: 8"

This large-billed finch spends most of its year eating tree seeds of maples and box elders. Some years, when the natural seed crop is poor, evening grosbeaks head south in large flocks and may descend on feeders for sunflower. Flocks are loud and gregarious, and the large evening grosbeaks easily stand out from the smaller finches at feeders.

FIELD MARKS
The adult male is mustard yellow with a dark head, bold black and white wings, a pale bill, and a bright yellow eyebrow. The female is plainer looking but shares the wing pattern with the male.

SOUNDS
Evening grosbeaks constantly call a loud, descending *pyeer!* Also a raspy whistled *pyrrrt!*

HABITAT
In its northern breeding range, deciduous woods. In fall and winter this species can turn up anywhere there is food, including feeding stations.

BACKYARD
Grosbeaks eagerly consume sunflower seed, especially white-striped sunflower. They prefer platform feeders. They will also visit water features.

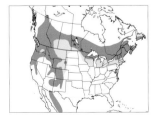

235

House Sparrow

Passer domesticus SIZE: 6¼"

This import from Europe was introduced in the 1850s and is now one of our most common and widespread birds, found everywhere humans or livestock live. It is a year-round resident across the continent, often outcompeting native species at feeders and for nesting cavities.

FIELD MARKS
The breeding male has a black bib, gray crown and face, and chestnut nape. Winter males are somewhat duller. Females are plain brown overall and lack the dark bib. The warm brown wings of both sexes show a single bold white wing bar. House sparrows are often found in flocks. They nest colonially in barns and thick shrubs.

SOUNDS
Song is a repetitive series of hoarse notes: *cha-deep, cha-deep!* Calls include *chirp!*

HABITAT
Any human-altered landscape, especially cities, towns, farmlots, and backyard feeding stations.

BACKYARD
House sparrows will visit (and may dominate) feeders for almost any kind of food. Some people stop feeding for short periods to encourage flocks of house sparrows to disperse. They will take over nest boxes and evict (or kill) cavity nesters such as bluebirds, purple martins, tree swallows, chickadees, and titmice.

Adult female (left)

Adult male

Resources

National Organizations for Bird Watchers

American Bird Conservancy
PO Box 249
The Plains, VA 20198
540-253-5780
www.abcbirds.org

American Birding Association
4945 N. 30th Street
Suite 200
Colorado Springs, CO 80919
800-850-2473
www.americanbirding.org

Cornell Lab of Ornithology
159 Sapsucker Woods Road
Ithaca, NY 14850
800-843-2473
www.birds.cornell.edu

National Audubon Society
700 Broadway
New York, NY 10003
212-979-3000
www.audubon.org

National Wildlife Federation
11100 Wildlife Center Drive
Reston, VA 20190
800-829-9919
www.nwf.org

The Nature Conservancy
4245 North Fairfax Drive
Suite 100
Arlington, VA 22203
800-628-6860

Field Guides to Birds

BOOKS

Brinkley, Edward S. *National Wildlife Federation Field Guide to Birds of North America.* New York: Sterling Publishing, 2007.

Dunn, Jon L., and Jonathan Alderfer. *National Geographic Field Guide to the Birds of North America.* 5th ed. Washington, D.C.: National Geographic, 2006.

Floyd, Ted. *Smithsonian Field Guide to the Birds of North America.* New York: HarperCollins, 2008.

Griggs, Jack L. *All the Birds of North America.* New York: HarperCollins, 1997.

Kaufman, Kenn. *Kaufman Field Guide to Birds of North America.* Boston: Houghton Mifflin Co., 2000.

Peterson, Roger Tory. *Peterson Field Guide to Birds of North America.* Boston: Houghton Mifflin Co., 2008.

Robbins, Chandler S., et al. *Birds of North America: A Guide to Field Identification.* Revised ed. New York: Golden Press, 1983.

Sibley, David Allen. *The Sibley Guide to Birds.* New York: Knopf, 2000.

Stokes, Donald, and Lillian Stokes. *Stokes Field Guide to Birds: Eastern Region.* Boston: Little, Brown and Co., 1996.

Thompson, Bill, III. *The Young Birder's Guide to Birds of Eastern North America.* Boston: Houghton Mifflin Harcourt, 2008.

MULTIMEDIA GUIDES

Audubon Guides
www.audubonguides.com

Handheld Birds from National Geographic
www.handheldbirds.com

BirdsEye
www.getbirdseye.com

iBird Digital Field Guides
www.ibirdexplorer.com

BirdJam Audio Software
www.birdjam.com

Sibley Guide App
www.sibleyguides.com/2010/02/the-sibley-eguide-to-the-birds-of-north-america/

AUDIO GUIDES TO BIRDS

Elliot, Lang. *Know Your Bird Sounds.* Vols. 1 and 2. Mechanicsburg, PA: Stackpole Books, 2004.

Elliot, Lang, and Donald and Lillian Stokes. *Stokes Field Guide to Bird Songs: Eastern Region.* New York: Time Warner Audiobooks, 1997.

Peterson, Roger Tory, ed. *Peterson Field Guide to Bird Songs: Eastern and Central.* Revised ed. Boston: Houghton Mifflin Co., 2002.

Walton, Richard K., and Robert W. Lawson. *Birding by Ear: Eastern/Central.* Boston: Houghton Mifflin Co., 1989.

———. *More Birding by Ear.* Boston: Houghton Mifflin Co., 1994.

PERIODICALS FOR BIRD WATCHERS

The Backyard Bird Newsletter, PO Box 110, Marietta, OH 45750, 800-879-2473, www.birdwatchersdigest.com.

Bird Watcher's Digest, PO Box 110, Marietta, OH 45750, 800-879-2473, www.birdwatchersdigest.com.

Living Bird, Cornell Lab of Ornithology, 159 Sapsucker Woods Road, Ithaca, NY 14850, 800-843-2473, www.birds.cornell.edu.

Online Sources of Information about Backyard Birds

All About Birds
www.allaboutbirds.com

Bird Watcher's Digest Backyard Birds
www.birdwatchersdigest.com (click
on "Backyard Birds")

Cornell Lab of Ornithology's Project NestWatch
watch.birds.cornell.edu/nest/home/
index

Hummingbirds.net
www.hummingbirds.net

The Hummingbird Society
www.hummingbirdsociety.org

National Wildlife Rehabilitators Association
www.nwrawildlife.org

North American Bluebird Society
www.nabluebirdsociety.org

Purple Martin Conservation Association
http://purplemartin.org

Photograph Credits

Glenn Bartley 113 bottom left, 124, 126, 130, 146, 150 right, 152, 157, 169, 172, 175 bottom, 175 top, 178, 182, 185, 194 top, 195 bottom, 195 top, 207, 216 top, 219

Cliff Beittel 1 bottom right, 23, 63, 113 top left, 114, 118 top, 119 bottom, 127, 144, 193 left, 213 bottom, 214 left, 220, 222 right, 223

Randall Ennis 117

Brian Henry 8, 102, 167 right

Maslowski Wildlife Productions 1 top right, 1 bottom left, 2, 118 middle, 119 top, 122 right, 134 bottom, 134 top, 162 top, 167 left, 174, 187 top, 191 bottom, 192

Robert McCaw 99, 170 bottom, 205, 216 bottom, 227 top

Garth McElroy 1 middle left, 118 bottom, 125, 139, 148 left, 151, 156, 159, 165, 170 top, 179, 186, 187 bottom, 188, 197 top, 198 bottom, 202, 203, 204, 206, 210 bottom, 211 top, 215 left, 217, 225, 230 bottom right, 231, 224 top, 226 bottom, 226 top, 230 bottom left, 230 top, 235 bottom, 235 top

Charles W. Melton 58, 94, 115, 128, 131, 133, 136, 137, 138, 140, 141, 142, 143, 145, 148 right, 149, 153, 154, 155, 160, 164, 168, 176, 181, 183, 190, 196, 198 top, 210, 212 bottom, 213 top, 214 right, 218, 222 left, 224 bottom, 228, 233

Arthur Morris/Birds As Art 122 left, 161, 162 bottom, 191 top, 193 right, 212 top, 215 right, 224 middle

Marie Read front cover, 24, 116, 120 bottom, 123, 132, 166, 184, 189, 200, 201, 221 bottom, 221 top, 234 bottom, 236 top, 236 bottom

Bill Thompson III x, 1 top left, 5, 7, 11, 13, 21, 22, 26, 29, 34, 35, 36, 45, 48, 49, 50, 51, 52, 53 top, 53 bottom, 54, 60, 65, 68, 69 top, 69 bottom, 70, 71, 72, 73, 75, 83, 84 top, 84 bottom, 85, 87, 89, 91, 98, 100 top, 100 bottom, 101, 105, 113 middle left, 113 bottom right, 120 top, 121 left, 121 right, 129, 135 bottom, 135 top, 147, 150 left, 158, 163, 171, 173, 177, 180 bottom, 180 top, 194 bottom, 197 bottom, 199, 208 bottom, 208 top, 209 bottom, 209 top, 227 bottom, 227 top, 229 bottom, 229 top, 232, 234 top

Julie Zickefoose 4, 6, 12, 17, 38, 39, 43, 47, 80, 97, 103, 107

Index